A
Handbook of
Contemporary Theology

A
Handbook of
Contemporary Theology

by

Bernard Ramm
Professor of Christian Theology
California Baptist Seminary

WILLIAM B. EERDMANS PUBLISHING COMPANY
GRAND RAPIDS, MICHIGAN

© Copyright 1966 by Wm. B. Eerdmans Publishing Co.
All rights reserved
Printed in the United States of America
Library of Congress Catalog Card Number: 65-28565

ISBN 0-8028-1159-0

First printing, March 1966
Second printing, August 1974

Third printing, April 1977

Preface

The purpose of this handbook is to provide the minister with a ready guide to the leading concepts of the major contemporary thinkers in theology. The center of attention is focused upon Kierkegaard, Barth, Brunner, Reinhold Niebuhr, Tillich, and Bultmann. Although Kierkegaard lived in the nineteenth century, his thought did not catch fire until the twentieth.

The use of German terms has been generally avoided. For the person who knows German they would be unnecessary; and for the person who does not know German they would be confusing. It must be conceded, however, that a good theological dictionary of German terms is something to be desired.

The standard for choosing the particular list of terms here given has been the desire to provide a handy reference work for the minister who is interested in contemporary theology but who either does not have the time or the background to understand all the terms used.

The italics within quotation marks are from the original sources.

—B.R.

A list of all the abbreviations used for the source materials of this volume is found on pages 139–141.

ABSURD

The concept of the absurd was introduced into theology by Sören Kierkegaard. Kierkegaard did not believe that there was absurdity in God. But the truth of God comes to the existent, i.e., to man in space, time, and history, and in the conditions of existence; and the truth of God, which is existential truth, can appear only as absurd to man the existent. Matters of fact and of science are not existential truths and therefore the category of the absurd does not apply to them. The category of the absurd is reserved for existential truth.

Another word for the absurd is the paradox. When the mind confronts a paradox, it repels it because it appears absurd to the mind. But precisely so is the absurd characteristic of existential truth.

Christianity has a specific absurdity, and that is the incarnation of God in Christ. Kierkegaard writes: "What now is the absurd? The absurd is — that the eternal truth has come into being in time, that God has come into being, has been born, has grown up, and so forth, precisely like any other individual human being, quite indistinguishable from other individuals" (*CUP*, p. 188).

The Christian faith is, therefore, not a rational philosophy that man perceives in terms of rational structures. To the contrary, the Christian faith at its center repels the mind because its central thesis is absurd. It is paradoxical. It is accepted by the leap (*q.v.*).

Reinhold Niebuhr follows Kierkegaard in the notion of the absurd. The absurd is that in Christ the kingdom of God has come and God's sovereignty is unexpectedly disclosed in history (*NDM*, II, 35). He writes further that "the final truth about life is always an absurdity but it cannot be an absolute absurdity. It is an absurdity inasfar as it must transcend the 'system' of meaning which the human mind always prematurely constructs with itself as the center. But it cannot be a complete absurdity or it would not achieve any credence" (*ibid.*, 38n). Here it is to be noticed that it is the man-made, self-centered system that repels the Christian truth and reckons it as absurd.

Brunner says that the affirmation that the decisive event of

7

all history took place on Golgotha is "unintelligible, absurd" to the rational being. "For the cross and its meaning . . . is unique, never to be repeated, and therefore far above all human analogies; it can never be understood along the lines of intellectual argument" (*RR*, p. 166).

Tillich and Barth demur. Tillich rejects the notion of the absurd and prefers that of the paradoxical (*ST*, II, 90-91). Barth writes that "the incarnation is inconceivable, but it is not absurd, and must not be explained as an absurdity" (*CD*, I/2, 160).

ABYSS

The term abyss is one of Paul Tillich's more important concepts. God does not appear to man in a perfectly clear, rational form. God is at the same time the Ground of our being and the Mystery. Beyond all man's reasoning about God, God remains the Mystery. As Mystery, God is beyond all reasoning and prior to all reasoning. The abyss is then the ground of our being on its negative side, in its depth beyond rational comprehension, in its threat of our non-being.

Because God as Ground of being is an abyss to the reason, God can be known only through revelation (*ST*, I, 174). This revelation is the mystery of the divine abyss expressed through the divine logos (*ibid.*, I, 159). Tillich's own definition is: "In mystical language the depth of the divine life, its inexhaustible and ineffable character is called 'Abyss'" (*ibid.*, I, 156).

ADAM (*see also* Fall)

According to historic orthodox Catholic and Protestant thought, Adam was the first man created, and through his transgression the entire race fell into sin. In general, contemporary theology does not so interpret Adam. It has been deeply influenced by Sören Kierkegaard's work, *The Concept of Dread*. Kierkegaard wants to get Adam back into the human race, maintaining that traditional orthodoxy keeps him out. Adam is outside of the human race in that he fell from a state of innocency into sin; but none of us start from such a place. Therefore Adam must be reinterpreted so that he is like us, and we are like him. Kierkegaard does this by explaining the fall in terms of a psychological structure that he can apply to all men. In the course of his exposition he makes the following comment:

"Even though one would call this a myth, one must remember that it does not disturb thought nor confuse the concept as a myth of the understanding does. The myth represents as outward that which occurred inwardly" (*ibid.*, p. 42). It must also be noted that the subtitle to *COD* is "A Simple Psychological Deliberation."

Niebuhr says that Adam stands for "the ideal possibilities of human life" (*NDM*, II, 77). He definitely takes a symbolic view of Adam (*ibid.*, II, 78). Tillich says that Adam is man's essential nature in contrast to Christ, who is man's new reality (*ST*, I, 194). He also speaks of Adam as the time of our "dreaming innocency," a state of infancy before contest and decision (*ibid.*, I, 259). Alan Richardson says that Adam is human nature before God, i.e., Adam is Everyman (*TWB*, pp. 14-15).

Brunner is of the opinion that "the historical figure of Adam of the ancients, and the pre-Copernican view of Time and Space are inseparable. When one disappears the other vanishes too" (*D*, II, 50). Therefore we must abandon our notion of an Adam in a Garden of Eden. Biblical anthropology is to be constructed Christocentrically, and therefore to know the biblical doctrine of man we must first turn to Christ (*ibid.*, II, 52). Brunner, however, does square off against Köhler and maintains that Genesis is not an etiological story about why women are afraid of snakes etc.; it is really about sin, death, and judgment (*Kirchenblatt für die reformierte Schweiz*, 41:26, 8 Juli, 22 Juli, 5 August, and 8 September).

Barth discusses Adam in *CD*, IV/1. To begin with, the entire account is a saga and therefore Adam is the name of the transgressor "which God gives to world-history as a whole" (p. 508). There was no Garden of Eden with a once-for-all transgression. Rather, "It constantly re-enacts the little scene in the garden of Eden. There never was a golden age. There is no point in looking back to one. The first man was immediately the first sinner" (p. 509). "Who is Adam? The great unknown who is the first parent of the race? There can be no doubt that this is how the biblical tradition intended that he should be seen and understood" (*ibid.*). "He has not poisoned us or passed on a disease. What we do after him is not done according to an example which irresistibly overthrows us, or in an imitation of his action which is ordained for all his successors. No one has to be Adam. We are so freely and on our own responsibility" (*ibid.*).

9

AMILLENNIALISM, *see* Millennium, Views of

ANALOGY OF BEING

The analogy of being is a great doctrine of the medieval or scholastic period of Christian theology. It affirmed that a cause leaves a trace of itself in the effect, so that we may reason from the effect back to the cause. God as Creator is the cause of the universe and therefore we may reason from the universe back to God.

This doctrine of the analogy of being attempts studiously to avoid pantheism. God's trace in nature is not direct or immediate; rather, it is indirect, analogical, proportional. It is a Creator-creation relationship that is altogether unique in the cause-effect relationships. But it is true that from the being of the universe we may reckon back analogically and proportionately to God. This doctrine is termed in Latin the *analogia entis*. It was defended with great skill and much vigor by Thomas Aquinas, and because Roman Catholic theology and philosophy of religion are generally pledged to the philosophy of Thomas, the *analogia entis* is an important doctrine in Roman Catholic theology and apologetics.

Barth has led a full-scale attack on the doctrine of the analogy of being. He writes: "I regard the *analogia entis* as the invention of Antichrist, and think that because of it one can not become Catholic" (*CD*, I/1, x). The reason for Barth's position is not far to seek. According to Barth, revelation is given out from the freedom of God and is therefore given sovereignty. It comes to man unexpectedly and with no prior understanding of its contours. This is in sharp contrast to the doctrine of the analogy of being, which claims that it can prove the existence of God and deduce some of the divine attributes. One cannot hold to a sovereign, gracious revelation and to the analogy of being — that is Barth's contention.

According to Barth the analogy of being gives man an affinity with revelation before revelation is given. It gives man an aptitude for revelation prior to revelation. Even though man is a victim of the Fall he nonetheless has this capacity in virtue of the analogy of being (*ibid.,* II, 37, 43).

Barth has two versions of a doctrine of analogy of his own. In contrast to the analogy of being he offers the analogy of faith (*ibid.,* I, 279). With reference to our knowledge of God he has an extensive discussion of its analogical character (*ibid.*, II/1, 225ff.). If our language had no correspondence with the truth of God it would be fictional. But by God's own freedom and sovereignty He uses human words to express the truth about Himself, and these human words are the analogy of truth.

Brunner, with reservations, comes to a defense of the analogy of being (*D*, II, 21ff.). God is the Creator, and therefore the creation in some degree must reflect God. This is a biblical doctrine, Brunner contends, and it cannot be written off as if it were entirely Catholic or Neoplatonic. The doctrine of the analogy of being belongs to the doctrine of creation.

But, Brunner continues, the doctrine is capable of perversion. Man in sin does not have pure eyes to see the truth of God as it is and so creates theologies that are full of errors. But even in these theologies there is a reflection of the truth of God along with the clear manifestations of man's depravity. If we see the analogy of being for what it is, namely, the sign of the Creator in His creation, it is an acceptable doctrine. But if we attempt to employ it to obtain a valid knowledge of God we err, for we overlook the depravity of man.

But can we appeal, as Barth does, to the analogy of faith? The analogy of faith is based on the analogy of being. Divine speaking is understood only in that there is human speaking. The analogy of faith is only possible when the analogy between human speaking and divine speaking is presupposed. Then in a special note Brunner directly attacks Barth (*ibid.*, II, 42ff.). He states first of all that the analogy of being has not played the immense role in Roman Catholic theology nor in Catholic-Protestant polemics that Barth assigns to it. Barth is correct in seeing the role that the analogy of being does play in Roman Catholic theology, but in cutting out the diseased tissue of the Neoplatonic doctrine he has also cut out the healthy tissue of the biblical doctrine of analogy. There is a difference between a natural theology based on the analogy of being and the biblical doctrine that the creation reflects the Creator. The former is not acceptable but the latter is.

Tillich discusses the analogy of being twice (*ST*, I, 131, 239f.). The truth of the doctrine is that the statements about God as the Ground of all being must be made from a finite segment of being. Such statements are valid because all being participates in the ground of being. This, however, does not mean that there

11

Analyticism

is a natural theology but only that revelation takes its materials from finite reality.

Austin Farrer states that the attack upon the analogy of being in Catholicism is specifically on the Thomistic formulation of it. "But the problem of theological analogy remains, and the critique exercised by modern linguistic philosophy upon the very meaningfulness of theological statements forces it upon our attention" (*TCERK*, I, 40).

ANALYTICISM, *see* Theological Language; Theological Positivism

ANXIETY, DREAD

There are three forms of anxiety. Normal anxiety is the apprehension a person has before a known cause of danger. A person awaiting serious surgery is in a state of normal anxiety. Neurotic anxiety is a sense of apprehension and fear where there is no definable cause of the anxiety. It is thus free-floating or irrationally fixed upon some object (e.g., a rabbit) or a condition (e.g., a high place or a narrow place). The real cause of the anxiety is an inner psychodynamic disturbance. We may, thirdly, speak of the anxiety of life itself, an existential anxiety. Contemporary theology is concerned with this third type of anxiety.

The pioneer in existential anxiety was Kierkegaard in his work *The Concept of Dread.* Lowrie, the translator of this work, admits that there is great difficulty in finding the correct word to translate *angst* (*ibid.*, p. ix). Hollander used "dread" and Lowrie follows him, but the more frequently used word is "anxiety." The Spanish use *angustia* and the French *agonie* and *angoisse.*

Kierkegaard attempts to reconstruct the Fall psychologically and make the Fall part of the calculus of existentialism. Man in the state of innocency is confronted with freedom. But man is also a body and a soul united in spirit. Spirit represents the existential dimension of the human self. Man can have dread because he has spirit; animals cannot experience dread because they do not have spirit (*ibid.*, p. 38).

Man as spirit is confronted by freedom. This freedom represents possibility and therefore excites anxiety. Anxiety is not itself sin, but it is the presupposition of sin. In the state of anxiety the existent is dizzy before the possibilities of freedom. "Thus dread is the dizziness of freedom which occurs when the spirit would posit the synthesis, and freedom gazes down into its own possibility, grasping at finiteness to sustain itself" (*ibid.*, p. 55). When an existent chooses some finitude for its security other than God, it abuses its freedom and posits sin. But this in turn prompts a second order of anxiety. The first order is the anxiety before freedom and its possibilities. The second order is that anxiety which accompanies men as sinners in their leap into sin (*ibid.*, p. 49).

Brunner, who follows Kierkegaard closely, speaks of objective anxiety as the anxiety of man under the wrath of God, and subjective anxiety as man with a bad conscience before God (*D*, II, 119). Niebuhr is also deeply influenced by Kierkegaard at this point. He says that Kierkegaard's analysis of anxiety is the most profound in the history of Christian thought (*NDM*, I, 182n). Speaking of anxiety he says: "In short, man being both free and bound, both limited and limitless, is anxious. Anxiety is the inevitable concomitant of the paradox of freedom and finiteness in which man is involved. Anxiety is the internal precondition of sin. It is the inevitable spiritual state of man, standing in the paradoxical situation of freedom and finiteness" (*ibid.*, I, 182). Niebuhr also reveals awareness of the discussion of care (*Sorge*) in *Sein und Zeit* by Heidegger.

Both Tillich and Bultmann have before them not only Kierkegaard's *Concept of Dread* but Heidegger's extensive concept of care, which is a species of anxiety (*Sorge, Besorgen, Fürsorge*). Tillich, accordingly, has much to say about anxiety. Anxiety is "finite in awareness" (*ST*, I, 191). It is an ontological quality and it is omnipresent. "The recovery of the meaning of anxiety through the continued endeavor of existential philosophy, depth psychology, neurology, and the arts is one of the achievements of the twentieth century" (*ibid.*) Anxiety "is the self-awareness of the finite self as finite" (*ibid.*, 192). "Being a creature includes the heritage of nonbeing (anxiety) and the heritage of being (courage)" (*ibid.*, 253).

Bultmann also has a doctrine of anxiety. It is man's feeling of not being at home in the universe. Man in his unauthentic existence feels threatened and seeks a security that he cannot truly find. This anxiety before life shows itself most clearly in the anxiety before death. (Cf. Franz Theunis, *Offenbarung und Glaube bei Rudolph Bultmann*, p. 38.)

Apologetics

Lars Granberg notes the difference between existential and neurotic anxiety (*BDT*, pp. 110f.). He sides with the Kierkegaardian tradition that existential anxiety is the product of the tension of freedom and finitude. It is not sinful, otherwise Christ's anxiety in Gethsemane would have been sinful. But man in sin misuses his anxiety and thus becomes pathological. The only cure for anxiety is a childlike faith in God and the creative use of anxiety.

APOLOGETICS (see also Eristics)

Barth believes that the explication of the Christian faith is its own defense and therefore he has renounced all apologetic activity. His early rejection of apologetics will be found in *CD*, I/1, 29ff., where he lashes out against Brunner in particular. It is a continuous refrain in Barth's writings that the Christian revelation is above all human testings, standards, or criteria and therefore beyond any apologetics or eristics.

Brunner has stoutly maintained in face of Barth's attacks the need for an apologetics. He prefers, however, the word "eristics" (disputation) instead of apologetics. Christians are not called upon to prove the faith. At this point he is one with Barth that the traditional attempts to prove Christianity at the bar of reason are abortive, for the Christian revelation is self-attesting. But he does believe Christians are called upon to answer the attacks of all sorts made upon the Christian faith and to show that the attacks are devoid of force. On this score he thinks Kierkegaard was the greatest Protestant eristic thinker. Although his system is contained in *RR*, Brunner does give us a condensed view of his opinions in *D*, I, 98-101.

Tillich believes that theology must be both kerygmatic and apologetic (*ST*, I, 6ff.). The kerygmatic function of theology is to present the eternal gospel; the apologetic function of theology is to present the relevancy of the gospel to its age. A kerygmatic theology that does not become apologetical becomes irrelevant. An apologetic theology that fails to be kerygmatic loses the eternal gospel.

Every culture, according to Tillich, asks questions and poses situations and it is the function of apologetics to speak to the situations and to answer the questions. Hence theology could be called "answering" theology. Apologetics "correlates questions and answers" (*ibid.*, p. 8). Apologetics is not a special

14

task of the theologian but part of his entire theological activity
(p. 31).

According to Bultmann there can be no apologetics. The
only statements that are provable are factual statements of all
sorts, and theological statements are not of this order. They
are rather possibility statements, and before them we can only
decide. The statements of theology are unverifiable or un-
testable. One simply hears the summons of God in the kerygma
or he does not. If he does, he enters into a new self-understanding. Presumably this new self-understanding is its own
verification.

APPROPRIATION AND APPROXIMATION

Kierkegaard taught that there were two divergent ways of
knowing. "For an objective reflection the truth becomes an object, something objective, and thought must be pointed away
from the subject. For a subjective reflection the truth becomes
a matter of appropriation, of inwardness, of subjectivity, and
thought must probe more and more deeply into the subject and
his subjectivity" (*CUP*, p. 171).

The process of appropriation, which results in the transformation of the knower, is the means of knowing existential truth,
or the truth of God. The process of approximation is the means
of knowing objective or scientific or non-existential truth.
Knowledge by approximation is always relative and unfinished.
In its own territory it is king, and Kierkegaard offered no
substitute for approximation for the territories to which it is
suited. But he viewed it as a terrible mistake to use approximation for existential matters. In these matters it is
wholly inadequate (cf. *ibid.*, p. 25). "If all the angels in heaven
were to put their heads together, they could still bring to pass
only an approximation, because an approximation is the only
certainty attainable for historical knowledge — but also an
inadequate basis for an eternal happiness" (*ibid.*, p. 31).

Existentialists uniformly make a distinction between how
we know existentially and how we know scientifically, e.g.,
Buber with his I-Thou and I-It distinction and Heidegger with
his existential analytic in contrast to the sketch (*Entwurf*)
of knowledge that science gives.

Atonement

ATONEMENT

In *CD*, IV/1, Barth gives an extended treatment of the atonement. He also has some material in II/1, 398ff., where he discusses the mercy and righteousness of God. The very specific section on the atonement in IV/1 is under the caption, "The Judge Judged in Our Place" (pp. 211-283). Three things may be said of Barth's view of the atonement, to comment upon it in a most general manner.

First, out of the various analogies of the atonement Barth chooses the forensic as being the best of the ones employed in Scripture (IV/1, 274).

Secondly, Barth is most emphatic in his doctrine of substitution, namely, that Christ died for us. He discusses this in four theses. His doctrine is that God totally replaces man, rather than represents him. A key paragraph is as follows:

> The very heart of the atonement is the overcoming of sin: sin in its character as the rebellion of man against God, and in its character as the ground of man's hopeless destiny in death. It was to fulfil this judgment of sin that the Son of God as man took our place as sinners. He fulfills it — as man in our place — by completing our work in the omnipotence of the divine Son, by treading the way of sinners to its bitter end in death, in destruction, in the limitless anguish of separation from God, by delivering up sinful man and sin in His own person to the non-being which is properly theirs, the non-being, the nothingness to which man has fallen victim as sinner towards which he relentlessly hastens. We can say indeed that He fulfils this judgment by suffering the punishment which we have all brought on ourselves" (*ibid.,* IV/1, 253).

On the same page, however, Barth makes it clear that he does not believe that Christ suffered punishment in the sense of the older dogmaticians, that is, that Christ suffered to satisfy the wrath of God.

Thirdly, Barth teaches that the Judge is judged in our place. The virtue of the atoning work is that the divine nature itself suffered on the cross. He writes: "Because it was the Son of God, i.e., God Himself who took our place on Good Friday, the substitution could be effectual and procure our reconciliation with the righteousness of God, and therefore the victory of God's righteousness, and therefore our own righteousness in His sight" (*CD*, II/1, 403).

16

Brunner repeats rather faithfully the historic Reformed doctrine of the atonement. With Barth he agrees that the basic analogy of the atonement is juridical or forensic. Brunner writes that "the law is the backbone, the skeleton, the granite foundation of the world of thought" (*TM*, p. 458). He believes that forensic terms are the original stock of any serious ethics (p. 465), and he finds that the Scriptures are filled with juridical expressions (p. 465n).

Brunner defines sin as violation of law, and he believes that any doctrine of the atonement must start with this serious view of sin. Therefore only an objective doctrine of the atonement will suffice. "The more serious our view of guilt, the more clearly we perceive the necessity for an objective — and not merely subjective — Atonement" (*ibid.*, p. 451). The reason for this objective atonement is that man is guilty. "For guilt is that element in sin by which it belongs unalterably to the past, and as this unalterable element determines the present destiny of each soul" (*ibid.*, p. 443). Therefore the only doctrine of the atonement that will suffice is that which is penal and vicarious (cf. *TM*, chap. 18).

Niebuhr's treatment of the atonement is regrettably brief (*NDM*, I, 54ff.). According to him, the essence of the cross is that it reveals the sufferings of God for men. The cross represents the paradox of both the wrath and mercy of God. But Niebuhr carefully defines wrath as that structure in the world which reacts against the God-implanted structures in the world. He believes that all attempts to rationalize the essential mystery of the atonement (e.g., commercial analogies, juridical analogies) fail, but their intention is right. The intention is to state the paradox of the justice and forgiveness of God. In God these are one, just as the Father and Son are equally God (*ibid.*, I, 56). Niebuhr further writes: "God takes the sinfulness of man into Himself, and overcomes in His own heart what cannot be overcome in human life, since human life remains within the vicious circle of sinful self-glorification on every level of moral advance" (*ibid.*, I, 142).

Tillich discusses the atonement in *ST*, II, 170-177. He differs from Barth and Brunner violently. In a most general way, he gives what may be called an existentialist interpretation of the atonement. In typical fashion, he gives a polite nod to the historical form of the doctrine and then proceeds to reconstruct it thoroughly and sytematically upon existential lines. For example, he will not accept Anselm's doctrine in the form in which Anselm presents it, but yet he admits that it is a great doctrine because it psychologically emphasizes the truth that we cannot feel forgiven unless our forgiveness is within the limits of justice.

Tillich sees the atonement as a dynamic event having two elements. It is both that which God does and that in which man participates. The heart of his doctrine is that God has always been suffering along with man in man's existential estrangement. This suffering comes to a particular manifestation and power in the death of Christ, where we see that we are atoned as we suffer along with God. Christians "participate in the suffering of God who takes the consequences of existential estrangement upon himself, or, to say it succinctly, they participate in the suffering of Christ" (*ibid.*, II, 176). Further Tillich believes that neither the suffering of God nor of Christ were substitutional.

Mention should be made here of Morris, *APC*. Working very carefully with lexicon, concordance, and comparative literature, Morris builds a strong doctrine of vicarious, propitiatory atonement. With painstaking work, he determines by the most concrete methods possible the meaning of the Scriptural vocabulary about the atonement.

AUTHENTIC, INAUTHENTIC EXISTENCE

Kierkegaard, the founder of existentialism, taught that man as an existent could exist the wrong way or the right way. In *Stages on Life's Way* he argues that the aesthetic and the ethical ways of life are the lower stages of life and that the religious is the higher. But he did not use any clear-cut terms to indicate what is the true life of the existent and what is the false. This distinction was worked out by Heidegger into the terms of authentic existence and inauthentic existence. "Man exists authentically when his original possibilities, belonging to his being as man, are fulfilled. His existence is inauthentic when his possibilities are projected on something alien to himself" (*ET*, p. 137).

Although every theologian who depends upon existentialism makes this distinction in one form or another, it is Bultmann who is most directly influenced by Heidegger at this point. "According to Bultmann, inauthentic existence is characterized by a perversion in man's relationship to himself. Man is at odds with, estranged from, himself. Moreover, he is tempted to let the separation between himself and himself become a divorce, to misunderstand his relation to himself as a relation between his self and a totally foreign being" (*KH*, p. 214). "Authentic existence is there characterized as freedom — man is 'free from himself'; that is, his relationship to himself is appropriate. He is at one with himself, hence his existence has lost its enigmatic quality; he has laid hold of his true existence in a new existential understanding of self; he is free for his authentic self" (*ibid.*, p. 215).

In the most general sense, inauthentic existence is the way of sin, of a lack of self-understanding; authentic existence is the way of faith, the way of self-understanding.

AUTHORITY

For a survey of present options in authority one may consult Robert C. Johnson, *Authority in Protestant Theology* and Bernard Ramm, *The Pattern of Religious Authority*.

Religious liberalism centered its doctrine of authority in the religious experiences of men in contrast to fundamentalism which centered it in the sheer inspiredness of sacred Scripture. Contemporary theology has moved away from both positions. To put it in a most general way, supreme authority is located in God Himself and the Scriptures are made a relative authority. However, the authority which Scripture carries is given a more precise interpretation.

We may note three different movements in contemporary theology which attempt to limit or define more narrowly the authority of the Bible. (1.) The authority of the Bible is in its *word-bearing* quality. Thus only where the Church hears the "word" in the "words" are the Scriptures authoritative. (2.) The authority of the Bible is in the great historical events of salvation which it records. Thus the Holy History stratum of the Bible is the part which is authoritative. Or, (3.) the authority of the Bible is Christological. The canon within the canon is Jesus Christ. He is the canon for measuring that which is authoritative. Thus the Scriptures are authoritative only in that they are Christ-bearing or Christ-witnessing.

Bernard Ramm, in *The Pattern of Religious Authority*, has argued that any monistic principle of authority is not sufficient.

Authority

The principle of authority in Christianity is really a pattern of authority. That pattern is the intersection of the authority of Jesus Christ, of the Scriptures as the revealed word of God, and the Holy Spirit in his internal witness to Jesus Christ and the Holy Scriptures.

Barth's discussion of authority is in *CD*, I/2, chapter 3, section 20. His discussion is a bit muddied as he spends more of his time rebutting wrong notions than explicating the right notion. Barth states that the only authority in Church that is direct, absolute, and material is Holy Scripture as the Word of God. It is true that the Bible is an authority in the Church because it is an *old* Book but this kind of authority is mediate, relative and formal. It is also true that the Bible is an authority because it has the form of a witness but in its form its authority is again mediate, relative and formal. Furthermore tradition cannot compete with Scripture as authority and Barth devotes twenty-eight pages of small print to a detailed analysis of the theological problem of tradition.

The Holy Scripture is an immediate, absolute and material authority to the Church in that (1.) God elects to speak through Holy Scripture; (2.) the Church is confronted by Jesus Christ in Scripture; and (3.) The Holy Spirit bears his witness in Scripture. All other attempts to shore up Scriptural authority by old orthodoxy, Neo-Protestantism or Catholicism fail since they come short of this criterion.

Brunner deals with the authority of the Bible in *RR*, pp. 127-130 and in *D*, I, 107ff. He first of all rejects the doctrine of verbal inspiration as the basis of the authority of the Scripture. His examination of Paul reveals the evident human factors in the composition of the Bible. "The divine revelation seems to be something which is freely appropriated in a natural human activity" (*RR*, p. 128). However, even though the Scriptures are in his view human and errant, they are the product of a divine inspiration. The purpose of inspiration is to preserve the essential data of the gospel even though this is not done inerrantly with reference to all types of facts. The gospel facts and their interpretation are secured for us by inspiration. The standard of interpretation is Jesus Christ, the Word of God. The writings of the New Testament "are human testimonies given by God, under the Spirit's guidance, of the Word of God; they have a share in the absolute authority of the Word, yet they are not the Word, but the means through which the Word is given" (*ibid.,* p. 129).

Tillich argues that the matter of authority is part of the dynamics of the times. At the time of the Reformation the authority for Luther was Scripture alone (*ST,* I, 47). Our times represent "disruption, conflict, self-destruction, meaninglessness, and despair in all realms of life" (*ibid.,* I, 49). Therefore our norm must be geared to meet this condition and that norm is New Being. More particularly this norm is "New Being in Jesus as the Christ" (*ibid.,* I, 50). This is central in Tillich and it means that the new, authentic existential existence is made possible by faith in Jesus Christ. In Jesus Christ the new possibility of existence has been opened up.

But how does this relate to Scripture? We cannot flatly assert the authority of Scripture because of the diversity of Scripture. With Luther we must introduce a principle within the Scripture which thus locates for us the authoritative stratum in Scripture. The norm which is derived from the Bible is New Being in Jesus Christ and this then is turned back upon the Bible to unearth the authoritative materials. "The norm derived from the Bible is, at the same time, the criterion for the use of the Bible by systematic theology. Practically, this always has been the attitude of theology" (*loc cit.*).

Tillich also discusses the issue of authority under the terms of autonomy, heteronomy, and theonomy (*ibid.,* I, 84ff.). "Autonomy means the obedience of the individual to the law of reason which he finds in himself as a rational being" (p. 84). "Heteronomy imposes a strange . . . law . . . on one or all of the functions of the reason" (*loc. cit.*). Theonomy is "autonomous reason united with its own depth (*ibid.,* I, 85). Thus the vigorous positivistic thinker accepts only that which his technical reason permits and he is governed by autonomy. The Roman Catholic believer in submitting himself totally to the Roman Catholic dogma and hierarchy is a case of heteronomy. Theonomy does not mean the imposition of the divine law upon the self but the self willingly identifying itself with the ground of its being, namely, God. However, Tillich cautions us that in this life there is no pure theonomy.

Carl Michalson finds the locus of authority in the apostolic witness to Jesus Christ made to flow again by the Holy Spirit. "Jesus Christ lives again in the spirit of man through the equilibrium of the apostolic word and the Holy Spirit" (*HCT,* p. 26).

This is not an imposition upon the self, for man's reason is created by God and is merely finding its original home. But theology must ever be critical because there is the perennial temptation within the Church to corrupt the principle of authority.

W. C. G. Proctor finds ultimate authority in God. But God in turn has exercised his authority through his Son. After his Son ascended He exercised authority through the inspired witness of the apostles, in the Holy Scriptures. "In other words, it is through the Bible that Jesus Christ now exercises his divine authority." But this use of the Scriptures as the authority of Christ is accomplished by the Holy Spirit (*BDT*, pp. 80-81).

Edwin Lewis finds God as ultimate authority but God has spoken his Word. His Word is contained in the Scriptures. Our authority is not the words of Scripture but the Word within the words (*BFCF*, p. 16). The Bible is not itself the revelation but that which revelation produces. "The so-called *authority* of the Bible therefore comes to light. Its authority is in that faith which created it, and to which it bears witness, especially that faith in its final Christ-centered flowering" (*ibid.*, p. 29).

Nels Ferré has treated the subject of authority in *The Sun and the Umbrella*. In the allegory which is the structure of the book, the sun is God as full, free, gracious out-going love and umbrellas are those things we allow to come between ourselves and God. Thus our final authority is God as pure, radical, free love. Jesus Christ, the Bible, and the Church are instruments to lead us to the sun. But when we take refuge in Christ, the Bible, or the Church we make them shades from the bright light of the sun. Thus the authority of Christ, the Bible, and the Church is purely instrumental in that its goal is to lead people out into the sunlight of the gracious, free love of God.

BEING, *see* Analogy of Being; New Being

BIBLICAL REALISM

Between the critical-liberal group of theological scholars and the conservative-orthodox there is a third group. This group does not see a sharp antithesis between biblical criticism and serious biblical interpretation. It combines a critical-historical approach with a sympathetic attempt to understand the meaning of the inspired text. Such a movement has been called biblical realism. It would include such men as Schlatter, Beck, Cremer, Von Hofmann, James Denney, the Mansons, Hunter, Cullmann, Otto Piper, and C. H. Dodd in his later writings.

From the movement have come new works in Old and New Testament theology, commentaries, and specialized monographs. The great *TWNT*, by Kittel and Friedrich, is in large measure a product of biblical realism.

BIBLICISM

Biblicism represents a strict program in theology, namely, the attempt to fasten one's attention exclusively on the biblical data excluding any help from philosophy or the history of dogmatics. J. P. Love finds the essence of fundamentalist biblicism in a strict literalism in hermeneutics (*TCERK*, I, 160f.). Barth gives it another interpretation in attacking the views of the biblicist G. Menken (*CD*, I/2, 607ff.). He regards a biblicist as one who wishes to read only the Bible and resolutely refuses to call in any extra aids for the understanding of the Bible. Barth's observation is that the biblicist attempts the impossible. No man can completely strip himself of conditioning factors and then read the message of the Bible without distortion. The biblicist is as much colored by cultural and philosophical factors as the man who knowingly uses philosophy and historical learning to understand the Scriptures.

Edwin Lewis speaks of the old biblicism and the new biblicism. The old biblicism was a static authoritarianism that identified the Word of God with the words of the Bible. The new biblicism is characterized by "inwardness, certitude, compulsion — these are the authenticating attendants of the Word of God, provided that the Word that controls is truly God's Word and not the words of men" (*BFCF*, p. 31).

BIBLIOLATRY

Bibliolatry is the unusually high veneration of sacred Scripture. Many contemporary theologians believe that the fundamentalists' view of the Bible as verbally inspired, inerrant, on all matters, and infallible in all its teachings is a case of bibliolatry.

Nels Ferré writes that "the use of the Bible as the final authority for Christian truth is idolatry" (*SU*, p. 39). Brunner comments: "The habit of regarding the written word, the Bible, as *the* 'Word of God' exclusively — as is the case in the traditional equation of the 'word' of the Bible with the 'Word of God' — an error which is constantly on the verge of being repeated — is actually a breach of the Second Commandment; it is the deification of a creature, bibliolatry" (*RR*, p. 120). Niebuhr says that we are guilty of bibliolatry when we make the Bible an authoritative compendium of social, economic, political and scientific knowledge (*NDM*, II, 152). We are also guilty of bibliolatry when the Bible becomes an instrument of human pride (*ibid.*, II, 231). Barth has virtually the same position as Brunner. To him the Scriptures are a witness to revelation and not the revelation itself. He writes that "we do the Bible a poor honour, and one unwelcome to itself, when we directly identify it with something else, with revelation itself" (*CD*, I/1, 126).

BROKENNESS OF REVELATION, *see* Revelation, Brokenness of

CHRISTOCENTRISM, CHRISTOMONISM

Barth believes that Schleiermacher gave theologians the concept of a scientific theology in that he attempted to regulate his entire work in theology from one principle consistently followed. He believes that the Reformers had this principle in the centrality of Jesus Christ but failed to follow through consistently in a scientific manner. Barth thus intends to take the Christocentrism or Christomonism of the Reformers and, using Schleiermacher's principle of coordinating all of theology around one guiding thesis, thus to write his dogmatics.

By way of example we may cite *CD*, IV/1. Barth makes it clear that he develops his anthropology (p. 348), his doctrine of sin (p. 362), of justification, sanctification, and calling (p. 147), of the resurrection (p. 283), and of the Fall (p. 478) on a Christological basis. He says that we cannot know a god in Christ and a god outside of Christ (p. 363). He very clearly spells out his Christocentrism when he writes: "But the programme of Reformation theology did not allow for a radical consideration of the meaning, importance, and function of Christology in relation to all Christian knowledge" (p. 366).

CHRONOS, *see* Kairos, Chronos; Time

COMMAND

In ethical theory both Barth and Brunner have taken the command of God as the fundamental of Christian ethics.

Emil Brunner develops his thesis in *The Divine Imperative*, chapter 11, "The Divine Command as Gift and Demand." In this connection he writes: "To do the Good for the sake of the Good is only a pale reflection of the genuine Good; to do the Good for the sake of God means to do the Good not because any moral dignity requires it, but because it is that which is commanded by God" (p. 121).

Barth has two major discussions of ethics. In *CD*, II/2, he locates ethics under the command of God, and in III/4 he deals with particular ethical issues within the doctrine of creation. It is in II/1, which deals with the doctrine of God, more particularly the possibility of the knowledge of God and the doctrine of the attributes of God, that Barth lays down his basic ethical theory. Ethics is usually treated in connection with the doctrine of sanctification or the Christian life, but Barth feels that from our knowledge of God there issues the command of God and therefore ethics must be located in our doctrine of God.

In sketching out the command of God as the fundamental of Christian ethics, he writes: "Ruling grace is commanding grace. The Gospel itself has the form and fashion of Law. The one Word of God is both Gospel *and* Law. It is not Law by itself and independent of the Gospel. But it is also not Gospel without Law. In its content, it is Gospel; in its form and fashion it is Law" (*ibid.*, p. 511). And, "For in virtue of the fact that the command of God is the form of His electing grace, it is the starting-point of every ethical question and answer" (*ibid.*, p. 519).

COMMON GRACE

The special grace of God is that grace of God whose intention is to save man. It is particularly revealed in the death and resurrection of Jesus Christ. It is also called soteric or redemptive grace.

The common grace of God is that grace of God directed towards man as sinner. If a man as sinner is to retain the rudiments of a civilization he must receive help from God, for having turned from God the only stopping point in the downward progression is total corruption. The only action that God can take to prevent this total corruption is an action of grace. This grace is called "common" or "general," to indicate that it is grace for all men, but it is not grace that has salvation as its intention. Its basic function is to preserve man from the ruin of sin by restraining the effects of sin and by prompting civic justice. Out of this restraint and prompting emerges the state with its cultural institutions.

Common grace does not, however, lessen the Christian understanding of human depravity. The Christian may appreciate art, learning, philosophy, culture and statesmanship in the unregenerate without compromising the radical need of men for the special grace of God. (Cf. Cornelius Van Til, "Common Grace," *TCERK*, I, 271-273).

Karl Barth rejects common grace, for to him there is only one covenant and that is the covenant of saving grace. If mankind is restrained in its sin and prompted in civic righteousness this is solely for the purposes of saving grace in Christ. God is not willing that any should perish and therefore God preserves man from total ruin that he might hear the gospel and be healed.

COMMUNICATION, *see* Indirect Communication

CONCERN, ULTIMATE, *see* Ultimate Concern

CONSISTENT (*consequente*) ESCHATOLOGY, *see* Eschatology

CONTEMPORARY WITH CHRIST, CONTEMPORANEITY

Kierkegaard was concerned with the relationship of history and Christian faith. He did not believe that a purely historical Jesus could be the object of a living faith. A believer could only believe in a living Christ. Kierkegaard gave this concept a unique treatment in *PF*. In the subtitle of this work he asks how an historical point of departure is possible for an eternal consciousness. His basic answer is that every man is contemporary with his own generation and with Jesus Christ. He discusses in chapter 4, "The Case of the Contemporary Disciple," and in chapter 5, "The Disciple at Second Hand." We are not contemporary with Christ in the sense of being eyewitnesses, but in the act of belief we become contemporary with Him (*ibid.*, p. 57). Being a contemporary with Christ means receiving from God the conditions for being a disciple. There can be no disciples second hand, i.e., by mere tradition or succession. In the moment of decision the centuries between the believer and Christ vanish, and the disciple becomes contemporary with Christ.

Tillich comes close to this idea when he writes that "no one is able to leap over two thousand years of church history and become contemporaneous with the writers of the New Testament, except in the spiritual sense of accepting Jesus as the Christ" (*ST*, I, 36).

Brunner also believes in the directness of the union of the believer with Christ, (*D*, I, 32-33). In agreement with Kierkegaard he says that there is no difference in directness between the apostles' knowledge of Christ and ours. The difference is in the means of witness. The apostles witnessed Jesus Christ directly, but Christians know Christ through the witness of the apostles enlivened by the Holy Spirit. All successive generations are dependent upon the witness of the first generation of apostles, but this witness makes Christ living through the witnessing of the Holy Spirit. "The revelation in Jesus Christ produces the *illumination* in my heart and mind, so that I can now see what I could not see before, and what so many are unable to see: that this man is the Christ. Suddenly, all the barriers of time and space have faded away; I have become 'contemporary' with Christ, as much His 'contemporary' as Peter was" (*RR*, p. 170).

Barth also has a doctrine of contemporaneity. He believes that the Word of God as revelation, as witnessed in Scripture, as given in proclamation is one Word of God. Therefore those who believe the Word of God are contemporary with it (*CD*, I/1, 169). "Where and when Jesus Christ becomes contemporaneous with us through Scripture and proclamation . . . we come under a Lordship" (*ibid.*, p. 170). In another volume he follows the note sounded by Kierkegaard that we actually become contemporaneous with Jesus Christ and therefore there is a directness in our encounter with Him. To overcome our temporal barriers is to be contemporary with Christ and this means coming into direct relationship with Him (*ibid.*, IV/1, p. 293).

COVENANT THEOLOGY

Reformed theology sees the drama of the Bible in the form of two covenants: the covenant of works made with Adam, and the covenant of grace between the Father and the Son. After the sin and fall of Adam the covenant of grace comes into effect.

All the covenants of the Old Testament are thus various forms of the one covenant of grace. Its final form is the new covenant in Jesus Christ as revealed in the New Testament. Thus the history and the theology of the Scriptures can be harmonized under these covenantal principles.

Covenant theology is vigorously opposed by the Lutherans and the dispensationalists. The Lutherans oppose it on the grounds that it destroys the law-gospel structure of Scripture, a principle fundamental to Lutheran hermeneutics and theology. The dispensationalists oppose it on the grounds that there are seven dispensations and several specific covenants — Scofield lists eight (*The Scofield Reference Bible*, p. 1297) — and the harmony of Scripture is achieved by the proper division of Scripture into dispensations and covenants; to mix or confuse covenants and dispensations is a major error of the covenantal theologians. (Cf. G. N. M. Collins, "Covenant Theology," *BDT*, p. 144).

Barth recognizes just one covenant and that is the covenant of redemption in Jesus Christ (cf. *CD*, IV/1, 2ff.).

CREATION

The doctrine of creation has received fresh treatment from Old and New Testament scholars as well as from systematic theologians. The historic view prevailing in the Church prior to the times of modern geology and biology was that Genesis not only revealed the theological components of creation but also revealed how God actually did empirically create the heavens and the earth. However, the recent mood among theologians and biblical scholars is that the two must be separated. The Genesis account is true theologically (e.g., God is Creator of all, Lord of all, man is in the image of God, man is a responsible creature, etc.) but the cosmological framework is dated and is therefore not a part of biblical faith. An investigation of creation in the Psalms, the prophets, and the New Testament reinforces this position. (For the strict biblical investigation, cf. *TWNT*, III, 999-1034).

Barth's treatment of creation is the most massive in the history of the Christian Church. He devotes four volumes to creation (*CD*, III/1, 2, 3, 4; basic theses in III/1). Barth does not regard Genesis 1-3 as myth, but as saga or legend, and, he interprets creation Christologically.

Brunner writes:

> The Christian statement on Creation is not a theory of the way in which the world came into being — whether once for all, or in continuous evolution — but it is an "existential" statement. In His revelation the Lord meets me, my Lord, as the Creator, as my Creator and the Creator of all things. In so doing I become aware that I know that I am the servant of this Lord, am His servant, His property, because all that I am and have I have from Him, because not only I but all that is, has been created by Him (*HAR, D,* II, 35).

Langdon Gilkey has produced a very thorough work on the theological and philosophical elements of creation. His central thesis is as follows:

> The Christian doctrine of creation, therefore, expresses in theoretical language those positive religious affirmations which biblical faith in God makes in response to the mystery of the meaning and destiny of our creaturely finitude. These affirmations are: 1) That the world has come to be from the transcendent holiness and power of God, who because He is the ultimate origin is the ultimate Ruler of all created things. 2) That because of God's creative and ruling power our finite life and the events in which we live have, despite their bewildering mystery and their frequently tragic character, a meaning, a purpose, and a destiny beyond any immediate and apparent futility. 3) That man's life, and therefore *my* life, is not my own to 'do with' merely as I please, but is claimed for . . . a power and will beyond my will. This is what the Christian means when he says, "I believe in God the Father Almighty, Maker of heaven and earth." This is what the idea of *creatio ex nihilo* is essentially "about" (*MHE,* p. 30-31).

Contemporary emphasis is on the following points: (1) The problem of creation and the work of the natural sciences are two different universes of discourse and should not be confused. Barth disclaims any connection between his theological exposition and the conclusions of science (*CD,* III/1, vii, viii). (2) Deeply involved in Israel's understanding of history is a corresponding understanding of creation. If God is the ruler of the history of Israel, He must be the ruler of the stage upon which the history is enacted, namely, nature or creation. Therefore the Lord of Israel is also the Lord and thus Creator of the heavens and the earth. To confess one's creaturehood is also to confess the Lordship of the Creator. (3) The New Testament doctrine of creation has a strong Christological element. Christ is truly God, and therefore He participates in the work

29

of the Trinity and therefore in creation. Barth uses this as a fulcrum to teach a Christological doctrine of creation. Creation is the external condition of the covenant of grace in Christ; the covenant of grace in Christ is the internal meaning of creation. (4) Each of us is to confess God as our Creator as well as our Redeemer. Denebeaux comments that the Reformers were so anxious to state the doctrine of the redemption and justification correctly they neglected the theology of creation. It took Kierkegaard to call man back to a recognition of his creaturehood (*HCT*, pp. 65-67). Niebuhr's comment is: "Faith concludes that the same 'Thou' who confronts us in our personal experience is also the source and Creator of the whole world" (*NDM*, I, 132).

CRISIS

In its earlier phase neo-orthodoxy was called crisis theology (Greek *krisis,* a judgment, a turning). There is the divine crisis, i.e., judgment, of God against man and his civilization, and there is the crisis of man, i.e., turning, in which man in faith turns to God in the hearing of the Word of God.

Crisis theology was also called dialectical theology because it used dialectic to sharpen the crises between God and man. For example, there is the dialectical relationship of time and eternity. Further, in contrast to liberalism's attempt to seek a harmony of Christian faith and culture, dialectical theologians saw God as sitting in judgment over all of man's efforts, individual and corporate. There is also the existential crisis of man's own involvement in the contradiction in his own life. Thus Brunner's *MIR* also carries in the German title (*Widerspruch*) the notion of man's being in a state of existential contradiction.

The Word of God precipitates the crisis. If it is heard in faith, it becomes the turning point of man to the life of faith. But faith is not a something, an achievement; it is a continuous and continuing response to the Word of God. Faith is always under the crisis of the Word of God and therefore is ever in need of renewal (cf. Paul L. Lehmann, "The Theology of Crisis," *TCERK,* I, 309-312).

DECISION

That decision is an element of faith stems from Kierkegaard. That which is capable of the ordinary, rational assent of the mind is not the territory of decision. If the mind is presented with a speculative system it does not decide for it but assents to it. So with matters of science. Theories are not decided for; in virtue of their verification they are assented to. If Christianity were a speculative system, we would not believe it in the decision of faith but assent to it.

But if Christianity is a paradox, an absurdity, a possibility, then a person does not assent to Christianity; he can only decide for Christianity. According to Kierkegaard, Christianity presents man with "the eternal decision" (*CUP*, p. 199). Kierkegaard also connects decision with subjectivity (*ibid.*, p. 115) and with the "leap," for the leap is the category of decision (*ibid.*, p. 91).

Tillich says that we can only decide for final revelation (*ST*, I, 152). Every decision is absolute in that it chooses among possibilities; furthermore, it takes the risk of courage to make such a choice. Approaching decision from another aspect, Tillich says that freedom expresses itself as decision (*ibid.*, I, 184). As soon as decision is made alternative possibilities are cut off. A decision is made by "the concrete totality of everything that constitutes my being" (*ibid.*, I, 184).

The concept of decision is deeply imbedded in Barth's concept of faith. His grounds are similar to but not identical with Kierkegaard's. The Word of God comes to man without preparation, anticipation, fitness, or readiness in man. Man does not accept the Word of God because it fits into any system or pattern or scheme; man can only choose the Word of God in the decision of faith. For, as Barth says, "since the Fall, to exist as a human being means to exist in decision" (*CD*, IV/1, 702). The important thing is that the decision of the individual is able to be identified with the decision of God (*ibid.*, p. 705).

Brunner follows Kierkegaard rather closely, so with him, too, faith is decision. For example, he writes that the truth of the encounter "cannot therefore be appropriated in one act of objective perception of truth, but only in an *act of personal surrender and decision*" (*RR*, p. 371).

Bultmann is also in the existentialist tradition. For him, too, we have no objective, testable or provable criteria for the gospel. Response to the gospel is not assent but decision. Man as an existential being exists continuously in decision. His life is always on the stage, so to speak. As man is confronted with openness to the future he is confronted with decision.

31

DEMONIC

Kierkegaard speaks of a "Dread of the good (the demoniacal)" (*COD*, pp. 105-121). To be a sinner in the bondage of sin is not to be demoniacal; to be in the bondage of sin is to be unfree towards sin. The demoniacal is just the opposite; it is to be unfree towards the good. The condition of being unfree towards the good becomes apparent only when the good touches the demoniacal. That is why the demon-possessed in the New Testament always cry out at the presence of Christ.

Niebuhr and Tillich do not follow Kierkegaard in this point. They define the demonic as exalting the relative or conditioned to the place of the absolute or unconditioned. Tillich defines the demonic as "the elevation of something conditional to unconditional significance" (*ST*, I, 140). Niebuhr writes: "The possession of the self by something less than the 'Holy Spirit' means that it is possible for the self to be partly fulfilled and partly destroyed by its submission to a power and spirit which is greater than the self in its empiric reality but not great enough to do justice to the self in its ultimate freedom. Such spirit can be most simply defined as demonic. . . . This absolute claim for something which is not absolute identifies the possessing spirit as 'demonic'" (*NDM*, II, 110-111).

Haroutunian estimates the demonic as follows: "In our day, after several centuries of eclipse, the devil has returned as the 'demonic,' expressive of the depth and mystery of evil in the world, as against the view which sees evil as either caused by physical forces or as willed malevolently by man. . . . So long as men try to think adequately about temptation, the devil will be acknowledged for what he is, the quasi-personal father of lies, allied with death and sin, and a power in the world which only the living God can and does overcome by the gospel and 'the Spirit of truth'" (*HCT* p. 76).

Brunner's basic thesis is that a doctrine of the devil and demonic can only be discussed within the central theme of the Bible, namely, redemption through Jesus Christ, the Word of God. Fundamentalists and any others who believe in verbal inspiration take more on than they can handle if they think that from the Scriptures they can deduce a coherent Satanology. Speaking positively, Brunner sees Satan as the necessary opponent of man and Christ, who finds his defeat in the cross of

Jesus Christ. Moreover, if there is no redemption from the devil, there is no redemption.

Brunner examines alternate theories that attempt to explain the evil in man without recourse to a doctrine of Satan, and he finds them defective, e.g., Kant's doctrine of radical evil, Ritschl's doctrine of sociological evil, and Jung's doctrine of the collective unconscious. His conclusion is that "because Satan is a supra-human reality, the work of redemption of Jesus Christ is a real conflict, and redemption is a real victory" (D, II, chap. 5).

Barth gives very little space to the subject. He says the very nature of demons is such that we must give them a brief, sharp look and then turn away. Demons do exist and we deceive ourselves if we think otherwise. They do form a kingdom of darkness analogous to the good angels. But they stem from nothingness, chaos, darkness, evil, and Hades. They are the opponents of the good angels, God's heavenly ambassadors. They hasten to destruction, to the hell God has prepared for them (CD, III/3, 519ff.).

DEMYTHOLOGIZE (see also Myth)

This is a term made famous by Rudolf Bultmann in his essay, "New Testament and Mythology" (KM). The literature on Bultmann's program of demythologizing the New Testament is so great that we must limit ourselves to the original essay itself. There is no substitute for reading the original essay (cf. also E; EF; JCM; Braaten and Harrisville, KH).

Bultmann believes that the New Testament contains the saving kerygma of Christ. But to express this kerygma the writers of the New Testament used the thought-forms with which they were familiar. These thought-forms were in particular the Jewish apocalyptic myths and Gnostic redemption myths. Modern man cannot accept the mythical and the Christian has no right to expect him to. But the temptation of some of the nineteenth-century scholars to reject the New Testament because it contains the mythical must be resisted. For inside the myths is the kerygma. Therefore the New Testament interpreter is to demythologize, i.e., strip off the myth from the New Testament and uncover the original kerygma. Thus Bultmann writes in his famous essay: ". . . does the New Testament embody a truth which is quite independent of its mythical setting? If it does, theology must undertake the task of stripping the Kerygma from its mythical framework, of 'demythologizing it'" (*KM*, p. 3).

Bultmann has a very precise program as to how this demythologizing and recovery of the kerygma is to be done. The real meaning of the myth is that it tells us something about human existence. But the science of human existence is the task of existential philosophy. So existential philosophy is the means whereby the kerygma is recovered. Bultmann's defense of the use of existential philosophy is set forth in an essay entitled "The Historicity of Man and Faith" (*EF*, pp. 92-110).

DESPAIR

"Despair" is part of the calculus of existentialism. It is the main theme of Kierkegaard's *The Sickness unto Death*. To despair is to be "existentially sick." It is only in existential despair that we seek the gospel and find the reward of eternal life. Kierkegaard writes: "Ah, so much is said about human want and misery . . . but only that man's life is wasted who lived on, so deceived by the joys of life or by its sorrows that he never became eternally and decisively conscious of himself as spirit, or . . . never became aware and in the deepest sense received an impress of the fact that there is a God, and that he, himself, his self, exists before this God, which gain of infinity is never attained except through despair" (*SUD*, pp. 159-160).

Writers influenced by Kierkegaard also have something to say about despair. Niebuhr says that the knowledge that God suffers for our sins drives us to despair, and despair drives us to contrition, and this creaturely despair induces new faith (*NDM*, II, 56, 207).

Brunner says that faith strikes only in the heart filled with despair, and in despair we stretch out for the help of the salvation of God (*RR*, p. 424). Tillich says that Kierkegaard's *Sickness unto Death* is the best description that we have of despair (*ST*, II, 75). To him despair is the state of inescapable conflict as well as the sorrow of this world that works death. No creaturely solution for despair is to be sought, particularly not in suicide. Despair must be solved on the basis of eternity.

DEUS ABSCONDITUS (*see also* Other, Wholly)

The concepts of *Deus Absconditus,* the Wholly Other, and the Hidden God are interrelated. For a survey of thought on this subject from Luther to present times see John Dillenberger, *God Hidden and Revealed.*

It was Luther who first spoke so much of these topics. Another important chapter was added by Pascal, who said that because man was a sinner, God had become hidden. Kierkegaard added another chapter by stressing that God is the Wholly Other, the Mystery. God is not known in nature, i.e., by natural theology. His presence in nature is secret. Dillenberger shows how religious liberalism, in the specific case of Ritschl, could not handle the doctrine.

Brunner is much indebted to Luther for his notion of *Deus Absconditus.* God in His holiness and wrath is a hidden God. This is the God man confronts if he attempts to search for Him in nature, or if he attempts to search for Him in his sinfulness (*D,* I, 161ff.). Barth has a similar doctrine when he emphasizes the mystery of God (*CD,* II/1, pp. 38-43). "Inscrutibility, . . . hiddenness, belongs to the nature of Him who is called God in the Bible. As Creator, this God is distinct from the world, i.e., as the person He is, He does not belong to the realm of what man as creature can know directly about God" (*ibid.,* I/1, 368).

DIALECTIC

Dialectic is a form of logic that men use when they are on their way to the truth. If we already have the truth, we make assertions by making deductions from that which we already know. In the language of geometry, we deduce theorems from axioms. But if we are on the way to the truth we are not in a position to make such deductions. We must *converse* to find the truth. The early Platonic dialogues are the classic models of attempting to find the truth through guided conversation. Guided conversation becomes formalized into a strict methodology, namely, of asking questions and counter-questions. It thus becomes a logic of proposition and counter-proposition.

When neo-orthodoxy first came into existence it was known as dialectical theology because it did not believe in the direct sort of assertions about man and God made by the older orthodox theologians and the more recent religious liberals. It believed that the divine-human relationship was one of tension.

It had an existential dimension.' The only kind of logic ade-quate for this situation is the logic of dialectic, with its Yes and No, with its assertion and counter-assertion. Thus a theological truth was not adequately met until it was formulated paradoxi-cally by way of proposition and the counter-proposition.

Brunner, Tillich, and Niebuhr accept dialectic in some form. Niebuhr gives examples of what he considers dialectical formu-lations of Christian truth. Man is at the same time justified and yet a sinner; history fulfills and yet negates the kingdom of God; grace is both continuous with and contradictory to nature; Christ is the ideal we ought to be and cannot be; the power of God works in us and is yet our judge against us (*NDM*, II, 204).

Brunner uses the word dialectical in two senses. Taking it in its original meaning as conversation he affirms that revelation sets up a conversation between God and man in which man as creature is respected (*RR*, p. 15). He also refers to dialectic as the logic of assertion and counter-assertion, e.g., between original revelation and present sin (*ibid.*, p. 25), between holi-ness and love (*ibid.*, p. 62), between our knowledge of God and our knowledge of sin (*ibid.*, p. 65), etc.

Tillich is very cautious in his use of dialectic, making it very clear that it does not concern the law of contradiction nor the structure of thinking. Dialectic has to do with the movement of being. Thus the doctrine of the Trinity is dialectical but not nonsense (*ST*, I, 56).

For further study, see E. P. Dickie, "Dialectical Theology," *TCERK*, I, 325-326; Bernard Ramm, "Dialectic," *BDT*, pp. 165-166.

DISPENSATIONALISM

Dispensationalism is the system of interpretation and theology contained in the notes of the *Scofield Reference Bible* and set forth in dogmatic fulness in L. S. Chafer's *Systematic Theology* (eight vols.). Although it has made few inroads into school or academic theology, it has received a large lay hearing through the *Scofield Reference Bible.* It is also the theology of a number of Bible institutes, Bible colleges, and liberal arts colleges.

The basic thesis of dispensationalism is that there are seven distinct economies of God in which God specifies certain con-ditions or terms and tests man for his obedience to these terms.

This thesis in turn becomes a principle of hermeneutics according to which one cannot properly interpret the Scriptures unless one knows the dispensation to which the given passage refers or belongs. Thus to put Christians under the Ten Commandments is wrong because it places under the terms of the law people who are under grace. It would be wrong to apply what is said in the Olivet Discourse to Christians, for the Discourse is about the coming tribulation, whereas Christians live under the terms of grace.

Application of this hermeneutical principle means, further, that groups must be distinguished, e.g., the Jew, the Gentile, and the Church. Israel forms a distinct group of redeemed people separate from the Church. If one pushes the principle further, a distinct eschatology develops. It is an eschatology that centers itself upon the future of Israel, her national conversion, her return to the Promised Land, and her millennial bliss.

With the seven dispensations there are eight covenants. The expert interpreter will not only keep his dispensations separate but he will also be careful to apply covenantal terms only to those with whom the covenants are made.

Dispensationalism teaches a twofold unity of the Bible. Along with the historic Christian heritage it maintains that the unity of the Bible is the theme of redemption centering and climaxing in Jesus Christ. To this it adds the dispensational principle of interpretation, and it does so in its efforts to harmonize the Bible. Moreover, it fastens on to a strict literalism, particularly in Old Testament prophetic passages. And it considers the application to the Church of matters spoken to Israel a cardinal error of biblical interpretation.

See C. L. Feinberg, *Premillennialism or Amillennialism?* (rev. ed.), for a sympathetic defense; for a critique and historical survey see C. B. Bass, *Backgrounds to Dispensationalism*.

DOGMA

Karl Barth has written more on dogma and dogmatics than any other living theologian. Nothing short of a book would do justice to the richness of his thought. An excellent sketch of Barth at work is given by Helmut Gollwitzer in *Karl Barth's Church Dogmatics: Selections*. The kernel of his views on dogma and dogmatics is as follows:

(1) The beginning and the end of dogma is Jesus Christ, the one, living Word of God. Hence all dogmas must have a Christological impress or they are not true to the central dogma of the incarnation of God in Jesus Christ.

(2) The source and norm of dogma is the Holy Scripture, in that it is the Word of God. But it is the Word of God in the very special sense that it is not itself revelation but rather the attestation to revelation. "The dogmatic norm, i.e., the norm of which dogmatics must remind Church proclamation, and therefore itself first of all, as the objective possibility of pure doctrine, can be no other than the revelation attested in Holy Scripture as God's Word" (CD, I/2, 815).

(3) The activity of dogma is an activity in the Church in which the Church reflects upon the correlation of her preaching and proclamation with the revelation attested of God in Scripture. It is a human, necessary, and continuous activity. It is human because it is man's reflection upon the revelation attested in Scripture. It is necessary because all the Church's activities must be tested by the Word of God. It is continuous because no dogmatic formulation is identical with the Word of God. Therefore the dogmatic task must be taken up again and again. Dogmas are teachings "which grasp and reproduce the truth of revelation only so far as they strive towards it" (ibid., I/1, 307). Hence dogmatics is always on the way of this striving.

(4) Dogmatics is not a corpus of revealed propositions but a series of behests, decrees, commands to be obeyed as much as articles to be believed. They are of such a nature that their inner meaning opens only to those who believe them.

Brunner also has a wealth of material on dogmatics such as D, I, 3-113. A short summary of his views is as follows:

(1) The ultimate source of dogma, dogmatics, and doctrine is revelation. The entire Christian scheme is built upon revelation and therefore all dogmatic thinking is from revelation.

(2) This revelation, however, is a Person, Jesus Christ. The center of Christian revelation is therefore personal. One may speak of the objective point of reference — the incarnation of God in Jesus Christ — as the final revelation, and of the subjective point of reference — the personal encounter of the believer with Jesus Christ. Doctrine about Jesus Christ must never take the place of the encounter with the Person of Jesus Christ. The

exaltation of doctrine about Christ into the same place as Christ Himself is the error of old orthodoxy.

(3) More concretely, this revelation is witnessed to in Scripture. Correct doctrine must therefore be Scriptural. But it must be Scriptural in a Scriptural way. Jesus Christ is the Lord and King of Scripture, and Scripture must be interpreted from this vantage point. To put it another way, not all of Scripture is word-bearing. The Word of God in the Person of Jesus Christ is the fundamental principle of hermeneutics whereby we exegete the word of God in Scripture. "Above all the teaching of the Church, even above all dogma or doctrine confession, stands Holy Scripture. This is the source of revelation for the Church; for the Church knows the fact of revelation simply and solely through the Holy Scriptures. Scripture, however, is not only the source of all Christian doctrine, but it is also its norm, in so far as the original witness is the source of all the testimony of the Church. It owes its normative dignity to the fact that the original witness itself has a share in the primary historical revelation, in the history of revelation of Jesus Christ. But the norm of Scripture, too, understood as the doctrinal norm, is not unconditioned, but conditioned: namely, it is conditioned by that which also forms its basis: the revelation, Jesus Christ Himself" (*ibid.*, I, 80-81).

(4) Dogmatic activity is, then, reflection upon revelation. It is reflection by a man who stands within the circle of revelation. It is not, however, "scientific" reflection, for the truth of faith is divergent from the truth of science. But it is responsible and clear thinking. It is also decisive thinking in that it wishes to purge out error.

(5) Dogmatics must be contemporaneous. That which is received is to a degree modified by the receiver. Thus the language, the concepts, and the philosophy of one period of the Church is not that of another period. "Substance," "essence," "nature," were vital terms in the patristic period but they are not now. The theologian therefore must undertake the risk and the necessity of translating theology for his own generation.

(6) The dogmatician must not be a system builder. Brunner is urgent at this point. He says that "rigid unity of thought, in dogmatics, is the infallible sign of error. Revelation cannot be summed up in a system. . . . A system always implies that the reason has forced ideas into a certain mould. . . . Dogmatics as

a system, even when it intends to be a system of revelation, is the misguided dominion of the rational element over faith" (*ibid.*, I, 72).

(7) Finally, dogmatics is an activity within the Church and should be Church confession rather than private opinion.

Tillich defines dogmatics as "the statement of the doctrinal tradition for our present situation" (*ST*, I, 32). He thus agrees with Brunner that dogmatics must be contemporary in its language and problems. He also concurs with Brunner that it is a necessary activity and an activity within the Church. But, according to Tillich, the terms "dogma" and "dogmatics" have picked up such harsh connotations that they are no longer serviceable. He therefore prefers the expression "systematic theology," in which he includes apologetics and ethics as well as dogmatics.

DREAD, see Anxiety, Dread

ELECTION

Karl Barth has attempted to give the doctrine of election an entirely new formulation (*CD*, II/2, chap. VII). He attempts to find a way that is neither orthodox Calvinism with its absolute decree nor watery Armininianism. His chief objection to the former view is that it makes the pre-temporal and therefore secret decree of God more determinative than the open and historical counsel of the death and resurrection of Jesus Christ. Thus the pre-temporal secret decree is in reality the deeper and prior word of God than that word spoken in the death and resurrection of Christ. The complaint against Arminianism is that it fails to do justice to the freedom and grace of God.

Barth's new way in election is a so-called Christological way. Jesus Christ is at the same time the electing God, the elect man, and the rejected man. Thus God's first word and open counsel is Jesus Christ. From this then springs the election of the community, the Church, and the individual, the believer.

Brunner also attempts to find a new way in election (*D*, I, 303ff.). He believes that historic Calvinism teaches determinism; and if we add to the doctrine of predestination the doctrine of reprobation, we get an iron-clad determinism. We can neither believe in nor love a God like this. But, continues Brunner, that which Calvin and company were trying to say is correct, namely, that God does elect in Christ, that man does depend upon the grace and initiative of God, that nothing in man merits his salvation. He defines election as follows:

> Thus it is this revealed eternity alone, through which, and in which, I, this individual human being, this individual person, receive eternal meaning, and my individual personal existence is taken seriously . . . in the Christian revelation of eternity . . . my eyes are opened to perceive the truth that God, *My Lord,* regards *me* from all eternity, with the gaze of everlasting love, and therefore that my individual personal existence and life now receive an eternal meaning. . . . The call that is addressed to me through Jesus Christ from all eternity calls me to my eternal destiny. To be called from the eternity of God to eternal communion with God — that is the Gospel of Jesus Christ. Briefly, that is the meaning of the New Testament message of eternal election, (*ibid.,* p. 305).

It is the address of the gospel to me through the Holy Spirit whereby "we *ought* to believe, we *are able* to believe, and we *must* believe" (ibid., p. 338).

Furthermore, the older doctrine had a false doctrine of causality and a false doctrine of eternity. Its doctrine of causality is that God treats man like a rock or a tree trunk. The biblical doctrine of causality is totally personal. The older doctrine of eternity spoke about a pre-temporal decree of God. But eternity is a dimension of present reality. From this eternity God chooses me and confronts me with the eternal meaning of my life.

Brunner agrees with Barth's treatment of election insofar as it disagrees with the older view and attempts a new formulation. But Brunner also disagrees. First, he argues that Barth's doctrine is so thoroughly objective that it diminishes the spiritual and personal character of the encounter of the believer and Jesus Christ. Secondly, he argues that Barth's doctrine that Christ is the rejected one means that no other man can be rejected, hence all are saved. Brunner states that the witness of Scripture is very clear that there is a day of final judgment with an eternal division of mankind into saved and lost.

G. C. Berkouwer attempts a contemporary defense of the older doctrine in *Divine Election.* He is sensitive to all the harsh things said about the doctrine, to some of the unlovely expositions of it by those who are within the historic Reformed camp, and to Barth's and Brunner's criticisms. Berkouwer attempts to give the traditional view a restatement that is thoroughly Christocentric, and that shows by rather lengthy expositions that the traditional view contains no determinism, no shadows, no dealings with a hidden and therefore threatening God, no lessening of the need for the gospel preaching, and no cause for uncertainty concerning one's salvation.

ENCOUNTER

Encounter is the face-to-face meeting of two subjects. Deep in the apologetics of Pascal is the notion that only as man is confronted by Jesus Christ does he know God. Theistic proofs and natural theology are to no avail, and they pale in the presence of the encounter. The intense Christological approach of the *Pensées* presupposes an encounter with Jesus Christ.

The same theme occurs in Kierkegaard even more emphatically. In that we are contemporary with Christ we can encounter Him. The "external" aspect of subjectivity, passion, and inwardness is certainly this personal meeting with the contemporaneous Christ.

Martin Buber explores the notion of encounter in his book *I and Thou*. He writes, "All real living is meeting" [or, encounter, *Begegnung*] (*IAT*, p. 11). There is the encounter of self to self, and of God to the self.

Although Barth and Brunner both make use of the category of encounter, it is Brunner who makes the most of it. In its own way the concept of encounter is the very nerve of neo-orthodox theology. Brunner writes: "In the New Testament faith is the relation between person and person, the obedient trust of man in God who graciously stoops to meet him. Here revelation is 'truth as encounter,' [the title of one of Brunner's books], and faith is knowledge as encounter" (*RR*, p. 9). The encounter is occasioned by the sermon or sacrament. It produces the Christian experience and the Christian certainty. In place of the certainty of an inerrant, verbally inspired Bible the neo-orthodox put the dynamic and saving encounter of the believer with Jesus Christ.

Barth speaks of encounter with the Word of God as "genuine ineffaceable encounter, i.e., not one to be dissolved into fellowship" (*CD*, I/1, 160). That is to say, it is the real meeting of persons and will admit of no sentimentalizing into mere fellowship. "Biblical knowledge of God is always based on encounters of man with God; encounters in which God exercises in one way or another His lordship over man, and in which He is acknowledged as sovereign Lord and therefore known as God" (*ibid.*, II/1, 23).

ERISTICS (*see also* Apologetics)

Brunner prefers the word "eristics" to "apologetics." He does not believe that there is a "bar of reason" before which Christians can appeal. This seems part of the very concept of "apologetics." But the Christian faith rests in the truth of the living God Himself, and particularly in His self-revelation in Jesus Christ. This kind of truth cannot be argued before any bar of reason. Brunner does, however, believe that we ought not to limit our work to preaching the gospel or writing dogmatics. The Christian is called upon to call his own generation into disputation. The word that expresses this disputational activity is "eristics."

The program of eristics is to prove that hostile attacks on the biblical message are "based upon errors, due either to the confusion of rationalism with reason, of positivism with science, of a critical with a sceptical attitude, or out of ignorance of the real truth which the Bible contains" (*D*, I, 98-99). The two best models of eristics are Pascal and Kierkegaard. Concerning the latter Brunner writes: "We may indeed claim that no other thinker has ever worked out the contrast between the Christian Faith and all the 'immanental' possibilities of thought with such clarity and intensity as he has done. Kierkegaard is incomparably the greatest Apologist or 'eristic' thinker of the Christian faith within the sphere of Protestantism" (*ibid.*, p. 100). Brunner's own apologetics or eristics is his work *RR*.

ESCHATOLOGY

Eschatology is, historically speaking, the doctrine of the last or final or concluding events that end time and commence eternity. In the past sixty years a number of different emphases concerning eschatology have emerged.

Futuristic eschatology is the belief that all the principal eschatological events are yet in the future. Events will occur more or less as they are recorded in the eschatological passages of the New Testament. This has been the general opinion of theologians in the past centuries. The more vigorous of the contemporary futuristic eschatologists are the dispensationalists who take eschatological language very literally.

Consistent consequente eschatology is the position of Albert Schweitzer and those influenced by him. In this view Jesus was a preacher of the End-Time. He expected the soon and sudden inbreaking of the kingdom of God and the end of the present historical order. The ethics that He taught is called interim ethics, for it applies to that brief period when we await the end of all things.

Symbolic eschatology is the view of Tillich and Niebuhr, who believe that the eschatological passages of the New Testament are to be taken seriously, but symbolically and not literally. These symbols inform man that he cannot find his realization in history. Present historical life will always be characterized by moral ambiguities and ethical obscurity. Thus the second coming is not some event on a heavenly time-table but a reminder and a promise to us that our happiness is trans-historical.

Teleological eschatology was defended by Paul Althaus in the first edition of his work on *The Last Things*. In it he argued that such things as the resurrection of the dead, the second coming of Christ, and final judgment are not events that occur at the end of history but events that run concurrently with history. Thus every generation is faced with eschatological Christianity, not just the last generation before the proposed return of Christ.

Realized eschatology is the theory of C. H. Dodd that the final eschaton has come in Christ. There is no future list of events yet to happen. The kingdom has come and with it eschatological realization. We are now in the eschatological kingdom. Another version of realized eschatology is that of Bultmann, who looks at the eschatological as a character of the kerygma. Life is eschatological when it is open to the future, when it is lived in the free grace of God, when it is love in obedience to the concrete word of God.

Inaugurated eschatology is the position of those who believe that there are elements of truth in both futuristic and realized eschatology. It is true that the eschaton has come in the resurrection of Jesus Christ. The entire scope of biblical salvation — justification, regeneration, eternal life, etc. — is eschatological. But the return of Christ and the resurrection of the dead remain stubbornly as events yet to take place; they cannot be swallowed up in realized eschatology. There is therefore the present inaugurated eschatology and also a future of real events in which history will be ended and eternity will begin.

ETERNITY

Kierkegaard gave to theology a new and unique definition of eternity. He made it a religious category, not a category of time. Man is body and soul unified in spirit, and spirit is that which mediates time and eternity in man. At the existential moment time is touched by eternity. The existential moment is not a moment of time but of eternity (*COD*, p. 79). He also writes that "inwardness is therefore eternity, or the determinant of the eternal in man" (*ibid.*, p. 134). Furthermore, inwardness or subjectivity is to be placed between time and eternity in time (*CUP*, p. 193).

Brunner discusses a similar theory of eternity. There is a continuum of time. At one end is time as conceived by mathematical physics. It is time as pure units of duration. At the other end is messianic time, which is laden with meaning. The historic time of individuals is lived between these two times. But in gospel preaching messianic time approaches us as eternity, and when we respond and believe the gospel we actually share in eternity. "Hence in faith Time is not simply contrasted with Eternity; it has itself a share in Eternity" (*D*, I, 317f.).

Niebuhr also comes close to Kierkegaard's understanding of eternity. Eternity is not the infinity of time nor undifferentiated being. Eternity "is the changeless source of man's changing being" (*NDM*, I, 124). "The real situation is that [man] has an environment of eternity which he cannot know through the mere logical ordering of his experience" (*ibid.*, p. 125).

According to Barth, eternity is the "time" in which God lives, in which the past, the present, and the future merge into the Now. "Eternity is the simultaneity of beginning, middle and end, and to that extent it is pure duration. . . . Eternity is not, then, an infinite extension of time both backwards and forwards. Time can have nothing to do with God" (*CD*, II/1, 608ff.).

Cullmann believes that Barth's notion of time is infected with Platonism. According to Cullmann the biblical writers see time as coming at them from eternity, coming to them, and then proceeding on endlessly into the future (*CT*, chap. 3). Thus eternity to primitive Christianity is "endlessly extended time" (*ibid.*, p. 65). See also C. F. H. Henry, "Eternity," *BDT*, pp. 197-199.

EXISTENTIALISM

Existentialism is a radical new departure in philosophy that was anticipated in Pascal and worked out more systematically by Kierkegaard. Pascal divided man's powers of knowing into two divisions, that of the reason and that of the heart. The reason has for its domain all ordinary knowledge, mathematical knowledge, and scientific knowledge. The heart has for its domain the territory of religion. The terrible mistake in religion is the attempt to resolve its problems by the use of reason. The heart, to the contrary, is subject only to its own laws. The heart is the intuition, depth-perception, and self-involvement in the knowing of the Christian gospel.

Kierkegaard, although not knowing of Pascal, develops his thought in every way. For Kierkegaard, too, there are two ways of knowing. The way of approximation is the means whereby man knows the realm of the objective, i.e., science, mathematics, the world of things and objects around us. The way of appropriation is the means whereby we as existents come to know Jesus Christ and God. It is a cardinal error to mix our ways of knowing. Kierkegaard's great contribution to existentialism was to spell out in much detail what this method of appropriation was.

The fundamental thesis of existentialism is that existence is prior to essence. This thesis means that my personal existence, my problem of being, my concern with my selfhood, my situation in the world is prior to and more fundamental than any theory about the world or reality. Man cannot begin with a theory of reality, a metaphysics or ontology; he can begin only where he is, as a human being in the midst of all the contingencies of human existence. To attempt to begin anywhere else is to attempt the fantastic.

If existence is prior to essence then any rationalistic approach to life or philosophy is excluded. We cannot find the mystery of existence no matter how hard we think and no matter whether we are idealists or materialists. Rationally we could know the meaning of life only if we stood on top of the universe and could survey it — which obviously we cannot; or if we stood at the end of history and could look back — and obviously we are not at the end of history. If we cannot think from the perspective of eternity, then we cannot rationally know the universe. Human beings as existents enjoy no such perspective; they are cast into the midst of things.

If existence is prior to essence then it is impossible to know the meaning of life speculatively. The mystery of existence is known only by the man who participates in existence. Kierkegaard writes: "What I am talking about, on the other hand, is something quite simple and plain, that truth exists for the particular individual only as he himself produces it in action . . . . Truth has always had many loud preachers, but the question is whether a man is willing in the deepest sense to recognize truth, to let it permeate his whole being, to assume all the consequences of it and not to keep in case of need a hiding place for himself, and Judas-kiss as the consequence" (*COD*, p. 123).

Around this fundamental position Kierkegaard develops such categories as the leap, the absurd, the paradox, inwardness, passion, and subjectivity.

In his analysis of existence, Kierkegaard develops a Christian version of existentialism. The eternal happiness that man seeks is found only in the incarnate Jesus Christ. He is the Supreme Paradox who excites in man faith as passion, as inwardness, as subjectivity. As existents we are not interested in true propositions but being personally in the truth. When we respond to Christ as God-incarnate with the passion of faith then we are in truth.

The two great twentieth-century existentialists, Sartre and Heidegger, do not attempt to formulate an existentialism from the perspectives of Christianity; on the contrary, they have developed atheistic existentialisms. Working from the concrete human being, *Dasein,* Heidegger attempts to spell out all the basic categories of selfhood, of the world, of the objects in the world, and of human history from the fundamental perspective of *Dasein.*

Although Heidegger comes to no theistic conclusions, his methodology has greatly influenced Bultmann, Tillich, and Ott. These three men attempt to use the conceptual framework of Heidegger as the point of departure for Christian theology, adding to this framework theological elements they have gained from Kierkegaard, or the Scriptures, or from their own convictions.

EXISTENTIELL

Some writers make a distinction between existential and *existentiell*. Existential refers to the formal analysis of human existence as such. Thus Kierkegaard's analysis of human existence or Heidegger's categories of the existence of the human being (*Dasein*) would be existential. But *existentiell* refers to man's own concrete existence and experience. Thus a man faced with a specific decision is in an *existentiell* situation (cf. *KH*, p. 174).

EXPIATION, PROPITIATION

C. H. Dodd has argued persuasively in modern times that the Old Testament sacrifices and correspondingly the death of Christ should be interpreted as expiatory sacrifices. Expiation is thus the forgiveness or removal of sin. The wrath of God is the consequence attendant upon our sinful actions (*BG*).

Two other scholars, Roger Nicole and Leon Morris, have examined Dodd's views and found them wanting. According to these scholars, Old Testament sacrifices are propitiatory: they satisfy the wrath of God. Thus the death of Christ is properly propitiatory. The wrath of God, mentioned 585 times in the Old Testament, is the response of the holiness of God to human sin and cannot be accounted for merely as that which necessarily follows in human history from human sin (cf. Leon Morris, *APC*; *BDT*, pp. 424f.).

FAITH

Behind much recent thought concerning faith is Kierkegaard's understanding of faith. He broke cleanly with the tradition that faith is assent or the acceptance of certain doctrines or the rational agreement of the understanding. To attempt to believe with the understanding is to believe about "livelihood and wife and fields and oxen and the like, which things are not the object of faith" (*CUP*, p. 208). To the contrary, "Faith is the highest passion in the sphere of subjectivity" (*ibid.*, p. 118). The sphere of faith is the paradoxical, more specifically, Jesus Christ, the Supreme Paradox. Faith is holding the paradoxical with the passion of inwardness (*ibid.*, p. 209). The goal of faith is the transformation of the individual (*ibid.*, p. 30; *PF*, pp. 47-50.)

Theologians in the neo-orthodox tradition are indebted to Kierkegaard's definition of faith. Faith is not acceptance of doctrine nor assent of the intellect but obedient response to the Word of God. Faith is the correlative of revelation (cf. *NDM*, I, 183; II, 25, 52).

In many places Brunner vigorously defends the Kierkegaardian definition of faith (cf. especially *D*, III, chaps. 10-18). One citation reveals the spirit in which he understands faith: "Faith means being gripped by the Word of God; it means that the person submits in the every center of his being, in his heart, to Him to whom he belongs, because He has created him for Himself" (*RR*, p. 421).

According to Barth (*CD*, I/1, 260ff.), faith is acknowledgment of the Word of God; faith is control by the Word of God. When Christ gives Himself to us as the Word of God, faith then becomes real faith. Faith is not a property or a capacity that man has in himself. "The possibility of faith as it is given to man in the reality of faith can only be regarded as one lent to man by God and lent exclusively for use" (*ibid.*, p. 272). "We have to think of man in the event of real faith as, so to speak, opened up from above. From above, not from beneath!" (*ibid.*, p. 278). "Man acts by believing, but the fact that he believes by acting is God's act. Man is the subject of faith. It is not God but man who believes" (*ibid.*, p. 281). That we should believe is a miracle. There is no point of contact in any formal sense; however, "the risen Christ passes through closed doors" (*ibid.*, p. 283).

FALL (*see also* Adam)

Kierkegaard attempted to give the Fall a psychological or even existential interpretation. He sketches out his psychological-existential structure of the Fall and attempts to show how Adam's Fall is the pattern for the Fall of every man. He maintains that the traditional interpretation of Adam keeps Adam out of the human race, and that he, Kierkegaard, wants to get him back in. By this Kierkegaard means that in traditional theology Adam alone commences from a state of purity and moves to a state of sin. But this is the experience of just one man on one occasion. Kierkegaard wants so to interpret Adam that every man in his own life and in his own way repeats the

Fall. Nor is he concerned if one wishes to call the Fall a myth (*COD*, p. 42).

The notion that Genesis 3 is a myth of a psychological-existential nature and not a historical account has had a wide hearing in contemporary theology. Alan Richardson writes: "The truth about human nature is enshrined in the biblical myths of the Creation and the Fall of Man . . . the myth of the Fall utilizes the tale of event in time . . . to represent a truth of man's condition that is independent of time and is an ingredient in all human living. It is a mythological way of speaking of an observable fact, namely, the universal human propensity to rebel against God's sovereignty by setting the self at the center of the universe, which is the place that God alone can rightfully occupy" (*CA*, pp. 131-143).

Niebuhr calls the account of the Fall a myth (*NDM*, I, 179). He says that we are mistaken if we in rationalistic fashion reject it, or accept it as literal history (*ibid.*, II, 267). The Fall is not history but "a symbol of an aspect of every historical moment in the life of man" (*ibid.*, I, 269).

Tillich has a very technical and existential interpretation of the Fall (*ST*, I, 255-256). He admits that the Fall is the most difficult and most dialectical element in the doctrine of creation. Man is created to stand within the divine life. But to achieve this finite freedom he wills to stand outside the divine life. But when he leaves the divine life for his self-life he separates from his essence and thus falls. Tillich writes: "To be outside the divine life means to stand in actualized freedom, in an existence which is no longer united with essence" (*ibid.*, I, 255). Further, this is the state of all men. It is hence universal, and being a "universal situation proves that it is not a matter of individual contingency, either in 'Adam' or in any one else" (*ibid.*, I, 256). Thus at the end of creation the Fall of man dialectically comes.

A. T. Mollegan calls the Fall a myth with a profound theological meaning. Furthermore, "the Genesis myth, and the idea of a 'fall,' can be used to express the human situation as it is experienced by both Christians and non-Christians' (*HCT*, p. 133). "Christianity uses the Genesis myth to express the fact that man's basic malady is sin rather than finiteness with its concomitant aspects of weakness, ignorance, and mortality" (*ibid.*).

Brunner's discussion of the Fall is consistent with his Chris-

tological approach to all theological problems (*D*, II, 89ff.).
Thus the first step in discussing the Fall is not to read Genesis
3 but to read the New Testament account of Jesus Christ. It is
from that standpoint that we come to the "myth-narrative."
Brunner says of this passage that "there is perhaps no part of
the Old Testament which impresses us so directly as a divine
revelation as the story of the Fall in Gen. 3" (*ibid.*, II, 89).
It is, however, from a knowledge of Christ as Saviour that we
come to learn our sinnerhood, and we bring this information
back to the Fall myth. Some theologians, in objecting to the
literal account of the Fall, have rejected the Fall altogether.
But Brunner will not tolerate this, for he writes that "every
conception of Sin which tries to establish itself without this
mythical idea of a Fall, proves, on closer examination, to be
an optimistic re-interpretation of the actual fact of sin, which
makes sin either a fact of nature, or merely the moral concern
of the individual" (*ibid.*, II, 90).

Barth calls Genesis 3 saga rather than myth (cf. *CD*, IV/1,
478-513). "The biblical saga tells us that world-history began
with the pride and fall of man" (*ibid.*, p. 508). Adam is not
a man but Adam stands for the entire human race in a state of
transgression. Hence Barth writes: ". . . the name of Adam the
transgressor . . . God gives to world-history as a whole" (*ibid.*).
The human race "constantly re-enacts the little scene in the
garden of Eden. There never was a golden age. There is no
point in looking back to one. The first man was immediately
the first sinner" (*ibid.*). Furthermore, the sin of the first man
did not involve the rest of humanity in sin: "What we do
after him is not done according to an example which irresistibly overthrows us, or in an imitation of his act which is ordained for all his successors. No one has to be Adam. We are
so freely and on our own responsibility" (*ibid.*, p. 509).

FREEDOM

Kierkegaard attempts to define freedom as an essential part
of the nature of man in independence from the Calvinist-
Arminian controversy. He views man as a body and soul
synthesized by spirit. Spirit is the existential potential in man
and as such is the source of man's freedom. Kierkegaard also
has a doctrine of possibilities. Man is not faced in the matter
of his existence with rationally compelling alternatives but

with existential possibilities. To be able to act on one possibility rather than another means that man is free. Thus Kierkegaard writes: "But freedom is the true wonderful lamp; when a man rubs it with ethical passion, God comes into being for him" (*CUP*, p. 124).

Niebuhr speaks of the concept of freedom in a different context (*NDM*, II, 1). He is aware of all sorts of determinisms that would make man a victim of chance or force. Although we must admit that man is a child of nature, Niebuhr insists that man is free and so transcends nature (cf. also his article on "Freedom," in *HCT*).

Brunner discusses freedom with reference to the image of God in man. The formal image in man is man's freedom and responsibility. When this freedom becomes real or actualized it appears as the love of God and one's neighbor.

Barth has written voluminously on freedom. First, he defines God as the God who loves in freedom (*CD*, II/1, 297ff.). Among other things, Barth writes: "But freedom in its positive and proper qualities means to be grounded in one's own being, to be determined and moved by oneself. This is the freedom of the divine life and love. In this positive freedom of Him, God is also unlimited, unrestricted and unconditioned from without. He is the free Creator, the free Reconciler, the free Redeemer" (*ibid.*, p. 301). Secondly, God in His freedom grants man freedom to be truly a creature before God. God has sovereignly limited His freedom in order that man the creature might have a freedom genuinely to be man. In discussing the freedom of man, Barth says: "Man is the one creature which God in creating calls to free personal responsibility before Him, and thus treats as a self, a free being" (*CD*, III/2, 194). Thirdly, there is no neutral doctrine of freedom. Freedom is freedom only when it is in obedience to the command of God. When man acts otherwise, he is in bondage and not in freedom.

Tillich does not agree with most traditional analyses of freedom and necessity. He thinks that the real polarity is between freedom and destiny. Freedom is not the faculty of the will but the function of the total man including the physical nature (*ST*, I, 182ff.). Freedom comes into play in three acts: deliberation, decision, and responsibility. But standing in polar relationship to freedom is destiny. Destiny is "myself as given, formed by nature, history, and myself" (*ibid.*, p. 185). Things have no destiny because they have no freedom; God has no destiny because He is freedom. But man has destiny, which is the basis of his freedom, and man's own freedom participates in the formation of his destiny.

FUNDAMENTALISM, -IST (see also Separatism)

Fundamentalism arose as a sharp counter-movement to religious liberalism. It sought to define and preserve the vital substance of Christian theology in an epoch of diverse theologies. Originally, a Fundamentalist was one who subscribed to the nine Fundamentals of the World Conference in Christian Fundamentals (May, 1919) or to any other specified list of Fundamentals (cf. "Fundamentalism," BDT, p. 234).

In the last two decades the word has lost precision of meaning. Theologians of a liberal persuasion may brand any person who is conservative or evangelical in theology as a Fundamentalist. Because a certain opprobrium has gathered around the word Fundamentalist other terms such as evangelical or conservative have been used. Thus we have the odd situation where the same person is branded as a Fundamentalist by the liberal and as a "neo-evangelical" (q.v.) by the Fundamentalists. It is therefore necessary to define Fundamentalism from a number of directions:

(1) As to attitude. Edward John Carnell prefers to define Fundamentalism as a kind of mentality (HCT, pp. 142f.). He notes its original vigorous stand for the truth and then its decay into an obscurantist and anti-cultural mentality. Thus a Fundamentalist is a person with orthodox convictions who defends them with an anti-intellectual, anti-scholarly, anti-cultural belligerency.

(2) As to separation. The Fundamentalist asserts that the leadership of traditional denominations has fallen into the hands of men who are liberal or neo-orthodox in theological persuasion, and he must take a strong stand against such leadership. This stand demands severance from such denominations and affiliation with denominations that demand and obtain purity of doctrine. Thus a Fundamentalist is a person who defends a separatist position.

(3) As to Scripture. Brunner defines a Fundamentalist as one who equates revelation with the words of Scripture, and accepts the verbal inspiration and inerrancy of the Scriptures. Involved in this is also a repudiation of higher criticism of both the Old and New Testaments. Thus a Fundamentalist is

a person who holds with obscurantism to the verbal inspiration and inerrancy of the Holy Scriptures.

(4) *As to eschatology.* Because there has been a close affinity between the Fundamentalist movement and the *Scofield Reference Bible,* a Fundamentalist has been defined as one who is in essential agreement with Scofield's eschatology of dispensationalism and premillennialism.

FUTURISTIC ESCHATOLOGY, *see* Eschatology

GENERAL REVELATION, *see* Revelation, General

GOD AS SUBJECT

The notion that God is Subject and not Object is suggested by Pascal's thought. His belief that God was not open to natural theology nor to the approach of the philosophical way suggests as much. God known by the intuition of the heart means that God is Subject, who only discloses Himself from His side when man makes the proper motions of faith. It is in Kierkegaard that the idea is broached more explicitly. Kierkegaard states that there is an objective way of knowing something and a way of subjectivity. Because of the very nature of God the objective way can never serve for the knowledge of God. Corresponding to God as Subject is our subjectivity, and only as our subjectivity is excited do we encounter God, the Subject. "The existing individual who chooses to pursue the objective way enters upon the entire approximation-process by which it is proposed to bring God to light objectively. But this is in all eternity impossible, because God is a subject, and therefore exists only for subjectivity in inwardness" (*CUP,* p. 178).

The same train of thought is to be found in Brunner. He defines a subject as follows: "That which constitutes the nature of the 'subject' in contradistinction to that of 'object': namely, freedom, positing and not being posited, thinking and not being thought, that which is absolutely spontaneous, that which is only active and not at the same time passive, that which only gives and does not at the same time receive" (*D,* I, 140). Thus Brunner is prepared to say that "God is Absolute Subject" (*ibid.,* p. 14; cf. also *RR,* p. 43). God is known only as he sets

54

the conditions for knowing Him, only as He reveals Himself, only as man knows Him in his subjectivity.

Barth also thinks along the same lines. "The subject of revelation is the Subject that remains indissolubly Subject. We cannot get behind this Subject. It cannot become an object" (*CD*, I/1, 438). The entire matter is explored by James Brown in *Subject and Object in Modern Theology*. He explores the thought of Kierkegaard, Heidegger, Buber, and Barth.

GRACE, see Common Grace

HEILSGESCHICHTE

This German word is translated as "holy history" or "salvation history." Although the idea was not completely new to Hofmann of Erlangen (being anticipated by Bengel), he is the theologian who put the idea to systematic usage and made it part of the terminology of theology (see Otto Piper, *HCT*, pp. 156-159; J. C. K. von Hofmann, *IB*; O. Cullmann, *CT*).

(1) *Heilsgeschichte* is first of all a reaction against the old Protestant orthodoxy that made Scripture the ultimate datum of the Christian religion. According to this view, the ultimate datum is holy history, and the significance of Scripture is that it is the record of that more ultimate datum. Scripture is the witness to the datum, not the reality itself.

(2) To those who hold the idea of *Heilsgeschichte*, a measure of critical treatment of the Scriptures is allowable. The antithesis between criticism and theology is false. The Scriptures may be subjected to a measure of criticism but never to the destruction of the essential fabric of holy history.

(3) Theologians of *Heilsgeschichte* treat Scripture as fundamentally the document of holy history. This means that there is a limit to scientific historiography. God acts in history and therefore holy history will have elements that are indigestable to the scientific historian. But this is the character of holy history — to be historical event and act of God at the same time. Furthermore, the chunks or pieces of biblical history are to be interpreted in view of their place in the total scope of holy history. The interpreter is to find out how each book or each section within a book serves the purposes of holy history.

(4) An interpreter knows the inside of this history only as he identifies himself with it. This he does by faith in Christ, by which he participates in regeneration. Thus the external principle of hermeneutics is holy history and the internal principle is the interpreter's identification with this history through faith in Christ.

Heilsgeschichte is used in a wide sense and in a narrow sense. In the narrow sense it means a particular scheme of interpretation of holy history, as in Cullmann's *Christ and Time*. In a wide sense it means the priority of the historical event over the Scriptures as the primary datum of the biblical faith. In this latter sense the notion of *Heilsgeschichte* has been widely accepted by Old and New Testament scholars. For a recent attempt to trace out in some detail a holy-history interpretation of both the Old and New Testaments, see E. C. Rust, *Salvation History*.

HERMENEUTICS

Historically speaking, Protestant orthodoxy has worked with three principles of hermeneutics. (1) It has accepted the grammatical or philological principle that was vigorously endorsed at the time of the Reformation but was not worked into a system until post-Reformation times. (2) It has accepted the psychological principle that the illumination of the Spirit is necessary for understanding the Word of God, and has done this on the basis that the Word of God is spiritual and can be perceived only by the spiritual man. (3) It has accepted the supernatural principle and has taken the miraculous in the Scripture as truly occurring.

Religious liberalism has accepted the grammatical or philological principle but has denied the psychological and the supernatural principles of orthodoxy. In their place it has put historical, cultural, and sociological studies. If the interpreter knew the environment comprehensively he could explain rather exhaustively the particular form of the biblical books.

There have been other alternatives for hermeneutics besides the orthodox and the liberal principles. One of these is interpretation according to *Heilsgeschichte* (*q.v.* J.C.K. von Hofmann, *IB*, and Bernard Ramm, *PBI*, pp. 79ff.). The basic idea here is that the Bible is the record of the history of salvation. This history within a history is normative for the biblical interpreter, and he uses this normative history in his exegesis of particular books or passages. The entire Bible is thus unified around the rise, progress, and conclusion of this holy history.

Bultmann offers another modern alternative in hermeneutical theory. He accepts the philological principle and also the historical and sociological principles. On the negative side he rejects all the supernatural elements of Scripture, and on the positive side he believes that a thorough knowledge of the times will go a long way in explaining the writings of the biblical men. More recently Bultmann has added a mythological principle and an existential principle. In his mythological principle he maintains that much of the New Testament is in the form of Jewish and Hellenistic myths. The task of the interpreter is to spot these myths and peer through them to the original kerygma. This process of going from the myth to the original kerygma is the process of demythologizing. It is aided by the existential principle. Existential philosophy gives us a description of the form of authentic existence. By using the existential calculus on the New Testament writings (which calculus is pure form), we may lay bare the essential content of the New Testament, namely, the kerygma.

Barth's hermeneutic is essentially a Christological hermeneutic (*CD*, I/2, 722ff.). For this reason he is accused of having a Christomonism. He divides the hermeneutical activity into three stages. The first is observation. By this he means nothing more or less than the traditional grammatical, literary, and historical approach to Scripture. The second is reflection. This is the mode by which the interpreter absorbs the meaning of Scripture. But this absorption is always through a philosophical grid of the interpreter, and so Barth discusses in detail the relationship of philosophy to theology. Philosophies may be used in the service of theology but no philosophy is the perfect counterpart to the revelation of God. Philosophical methods must always be judged by the Word of God. Finally there is appropriation. Here the interpreter identifies himself with the witness of Scripture. But in Barth's over-all strategy the Christological principle reigns supreme, namely, that Jesus Christ is the clarity of Scripture and the clarity of every doctrine of Scripture.

The views of Schleiermacher and Dilthey are receiving a contemporary hearing. Both of these men approve what is good in the philological method but add to it a psychological principle. An ancient text will not yield its meaning until the interpreter can find himself in imaginative rapport with the ancient author. Thus for technical details man knows (*wissen*) the ancient text, but only by psychological rapport does he undersand (*verstehen*) the ancient text (cf. Erich Dinkler, *HCT*, pp. 160-162). This method is being carried even further by such men as Fuchs and Ebeling. These men see hermeneutics buried in the very process of speech itself. They attempt to formulate a theory of speech that will bear the hermeneutical theory, and thus they speak of "Word-Event" and "Word-Occurrence."

HISTORICAL JESUS

One of the persistent theological and critical questions of the nineteenth century was whether the Jesus of the Synoptic Gospels and the Christ of the theological creeds were one and the same person. The conservative scholars believed that the Jesus of the historical record and the Christ of faith were the same person, whereas the critical scholars believed that the Jesus of history was very different from the Christ we encounter in the creedal formulations. The critical struggle with the life of Jesus in the nineteenth century was summarized definitively by Albert Schweitzer in his *The Quest of the Historical Jesus*. A solution to the problem that was not fully appreciated when it was written but has come into wider acceptance recently was that of Martin Kähler (*The So-called Historical Jesus and the Historical, Biblical Christ*). His thesis was that the Gospels were from the start kerygmatic and therefore the historical Jesus is one with the Christ of faith and creed.

The neo-orthodox theologians took a view exactly opposite that of the nineteenth-century liberals. Whereas the latter attempted to recover the original Jesus under theological debris, the former simply proclaimed outright that faith was interested only in the theological Christ. Attempts to unearth the historical Jesus were meaningless.

In the meantime Bultmann had been writing both critical and theological materials. In criticism he reduced our knowledge of the historical Jesus almost to zero, and in theology he made the act of God in Jesus the most decisive of all history and the very foundation of the Christian Church. Scholars were not slow in pointing out that Bultmann had reduced Christ to a mere "X", and yet maintained that this "X" is the very foundation stone of the kerygma and Christian Church.

Relief from this embarrassment could only be had if more could be said of Jesus Christ than Bultmann had apparently said. This opened up what is known either as "the new quest" or the "post-Bultmannian" period of Gospel criticism. It is an effort to find out by means of vigorous historical methods how much of the sayings and deeds of Jesus Christ we can ascertain as historically valid, and by such methods to increase our knowledge of the Christ who is the center of our Christian kerygma and Christian Church.

The literature, pro and con, that has grown up is enormous, and it continues to be produced. At the time of its writing, James Robinson's *A New Quest of the Historical Jesus* contained the important works in this controversy. For the story simply and factually told see R. H. Fuller, *The New Testament in Current Study*, chapter 3, "The New Quest of the Historical Jesus." Or one can consult the essay by N. A. Dahl, "The Problem of the Historical Jesus" (*KH*).

HISTORICISM

Historicism is one of the developments in the science of history during the nineteenth century. "The basic thesis of historicism," writes Hans Meyerhoff "is quite simple: The subject matter of history is human life in its totality and multiplicity. It is the historian's aim to portray the bewildering, unsystematic variety of historical forms — peoples, nations, cultures, customs, institutions, songs, myths, and thoughts — in their unique, living expressions and in the process of continuous growth and transformation" (*PHOT*, p. 10).

Runes' *Dictionary of Philosophy* defines historicism as "the view that the history of anything is a sufficient explanation of it, that the values of anything can be accounted for through the discovery of its origins, that the nature of anything is entirely comprehended in its development. . . . The doctrine which discounts the fallaciousness of the historical fallacy" (p. 127). Eisler's *Handwörterbuch der Philosophie* (second edition) defines it as "the tendency to observe the spiritual structures or cultural structures . . . as the product of historical evolution or to judge and evaluate them as historically conditioned and changeable; which denies the super-historical of obedience to law, or postulates norms which are in essence rooted in the spiritual life, or in the common experience of life" (p. 274). The article on "Scepticism" in the *Encyclopedia Britannica* treats historicism as a form of scepticism (XX, 59).

When historicism is applied to the history of Israel, the life of Christ, and the history of the Christian Church recorded in the book of Acts, everything normative, unique, or supernatural is dissolved. According to its postulates, if the historian knew exhaustively the conditions present in the ancient world, he could completely account for the rise of Jesus Christ and the Christian Church.

In reaction to late nineteenth-century and early twentieth-century historicism, much contemporary theology is concerned with showing how Christianity escapes historicism. Brunner does this when he says that the history of salvation is the history of revelation. Barth does it when he says that revelation is not a predicate of history, but history is a predicate of revelation. Cullmann does it with his history of the redemptive line. Followers of Von Hofmann attempt it with their theory of holy history. Bultmann has much sympathy with historicism but says that historicism does not reckon with the concrete decisions to which human beings are called (*HE*, pp. 141ff.).

HISTORICITY

Historicity is a term special to Bultmann. It is equivalent to creaturehood. It means that man is open to the future; that man is always on the way; that man is never the possessor of the certain; that man is confronted by concrete possibilities. In this openness and in these possibilities man comes to concrete decision. And in coming to concrete decision he realizes himself.

It is historicity that differentiates man from animals. In a given situation an animal makes a typical or instinctive response; man makes a free decision. Historicity is also the escape from historicism. Historicism wishes to catch all in a causal net, but man is free to choose among the concrete possibilities that confront him and so he is not caught in a causal net (*HE*, pp. 43, 46, 136, 143f.).

HISTORY, PRIMAL, see Primal History

I AND THOU

Martin Buber's little volume, *I and Thou*, has perhaps been cited more than any other book in contemporary theology (see the interesting essay on the book and its contents in Will Herberg's introduction to *The Writings of Martin Buber*). The basic thesis of the book is that there are two discrete ways of knowing. There is the world of persons and the world of objects. Persons know persons by the I-Thou relationship. The "I-Thou" is to be treated as one word. This is a primary word and is knowledge by meeting or encounter. The knowledge of objects is indicated by the primary and relational word, I-It. This is concerned with the total range of scientific or impersonal knowledge. It is the territory of information.

When we come to God we must say Thou-I, for the divine person knows us.

Buber is frequently listed with the existentialists as representing Jewish existentialism. His influence on Christian theology has been enormous. Brunner is deeply indebted to Buber (e.g., *RR*, p. 36 and *D*, II, v, where he says the I-Thou epistemology of Ebner and Buber is a Copernican Revolution in the history of thought). Barth repeatedly uses the I-Thou and the Thou-I expressions and greatly praises Buber for having taught modern man to rediscover his neighbor (cf. also M. S. Friedman, *HCT*, pp. 173-176).

IMAGE OF GOD

Kierkegaard wrote that "essentially it is the God-relationship that makes a man a man" (*CUP*, p. 219). This is a relational definition of man, and it has sparked a controversy over the nature of the image of God in man. (For a historical survey, including the present controversy, see David Cairns, *IGM*.) The principle controversy has been between Barth and Brunner.

According to Brunner, the image of God is fundamentally relational (*D*, II, 59). If the image of God is interpreted as a substance or a spirit, the image is made into something that man possesses of himself. Man's fundamental relationship to God is the relationship of freedom in responsibility. This relationship he has in virtue of creation. This is the formal image of God in man.

This freedom has a certain content intended. That content is man's love for God and his neighbor. This love for God and neighbor is the material image of God in man. Man as sinner does not love God or his neighbor, and therefore he has lost the material image. But he is still God's creature and therefore still responsible before God: he retains the formal image; sin cannot negate the formal image.

In hearing the Word of God in Jesus Christ, man believes and is redeemed. As a redeemed man he now loves God and his neighbor, and therefore the material image is restored.

It is, however, necessary to keep these distinctions. Brunner writes: "It is evident that our thought will become terribly muddled if the two ideas of the *Imago Dei* — the 'formal' and 'structural' one of the Old Testament, and the 'material' one of the New Testament — are either confused with one another, or treated as identical" (*ibid.*).

Furthermore, there is no distinction of formal and material with God, as strange as it may seem. God desires that the man who has the formal image of freedom in responsibility use this freedom to love Him. God envisions no alternatives. So if a man does not love God this is not an alternative that God approves or counts as a possibility.

Barth's doctrine of the image of God revolves around three ideas. The first is that of the man-woman relationship. The man-woman relationship is a reflection of the interpersonal relationships in the Trinity. The close association of man's being in the image of God and his being male and female suggests as much. When God said "let us," He was speaking within the Trinity of Persons. True, there are immense differences between the inter-trinitarian relationships and the man-woman relationship, but the closest human relationship to the Trinity is the man-woman relationship. From this we move to the concept that man's being in the image of God is relational.

Secondly, man is in the image of God in that he hears the Word of God and responds to it. It is the believing response to the Word that constitutes the relationship that in turn constitutes the image of God.

Thirdly, the real image of God is the human nature of Jesus Christ. He is the man of God's own choosing, and the man who is for all other men. Therefore He reflects perfectly the image of God. Furthermore, God has elected all men in Christ, so that all men are thus Christologically confronted by God.

Cairns points out the many problems with this view. For example, if men were born before Christ or never heard the word of God how can they be in the image of God? Barth's answer seems to be that sin cannot destroy the image of God; it persists in spite of sin. Thus sin does not make man inhuman or less than human. There must be secret ways in which either Christ is known or the word of God is heard so that all men are in the image of God. Cairns thinks this is a great imponderable in Barth's thought. Even so, Cairns judges that Barth's treatment of man will be considered "one of the greatest theological works of the last half-century" (*IGM*, p. 179).

Cairns then summarizes the agreements and differences of Brunner and Barth. They agree in that: (1) the image is relational, relational with reference to God and man. (2) The image is universal. Sin has not destroyed it. With Brunner it is universal through the formal image; with Barth it is universal through the man-woman confrontation. (3) Both of them construct a Christological anthropology rather than working with a philosophical one or one derived from natural theology.

They differ in the following points: (1) Brunner believes that all men are related to God through the Word of creation (i.e., general revelation); Barth denies this. (2) Brunner believes that in creation God gave man freedom, the freedom of responsibility. According to Barth, freedom is only freedom when it is obedience to the word of God. There is no freedom of alternate choices. (3) Brunner accepts a formal and a material aspect of the image. Barth denies this distinction. He sees one image of God, which is reflected in the man-woman relationship but fully realized in Jesus Christ. (4) Brunner sees the importance of the image for man's relationship to his neighbor in that the image is relational in this direction too; Barth sees it in the man-woman relationship.

Tillich believes that man is in the image of God in virtue of his reason (*ST*, I, 259), reason, however, not in the technical sense but rather in the larger ontological sense. Reason is the structure of freedom and "man is the image of God because in him the ontological elements are complete and united on a creaturely basis, just as they are complete and united in God as the creative ground. Man is the image of God because his *logos* is analogous to the divine *logos*, so that the divine *logos* can appear as man without destroying the humanity of man" (*ibid.*).

G. C. Berkouwer emphasizes that it is the total man who is in the image of God. He writes: "The characteristic of the Biblical

63

view lies precisely in this, that man appears as related to God in all his creaturely relationships. The Biblical portrayal of man . . . also emphasizes that this relation to God is not something added to his humanness; his humanness depends on this relation" (*Man: The Image of God*, pp. 195f.). Berkouwer cautions us not to look in Scripture for an exact, scientific psychology. In Scripture we are always confronted with the total man in the totality of his relationships towards God.

IMAGES OF REVELATION, see Revelation, Images of

IMMANENCE

P. K. Jewett has defined immanence as "that view which regards man and God as metaphysically, epistemologically and ethically continuous, so that man may arrive at the true knowledge of God within the framework of his own possibilities" (*BCR*, p. 12). The theology of religious liberalism was a theology of divine immanence. Total divine immanence is pantheism and the leaven of pantheism has been found in Schleiermacher, the first great theologian of religious liberalism. Some of the theological liberals were aware of this pantheistic leaven and sought to avoid it by speaking of pan-en-theism — God in all things. One of the basic premises of religious liberalism is *continuity*. Continuity contrasts with the discontinuities of orthodox supernaturalism (cf. Cauthen, *IARL*, pp. 6ff.). This concept of continuity is none other than that of divine immanence, especially in its thorough application to all theological topics.

The doctrine of divine immanence was in principle rejected by Pascal in his doctrine of *Deus Incognito*. If God is in hiding He is not immanent. It was struck a powerful blow in the theology of Kierkegaard, who wrote that "there is an endless yawning difference between God and man" (Bretall, *KA*, p. 409). Kierkegaard also said that if "God exists [He] is distinguished by an infinite difference of quality from all that it means to be man" (*ibid.*, p. 391).

It was under the impulse of this last citation of Kierkegaard that Barth wrote the second edition of his *Epistle to the Romans*. Barth's great doctrine of God is dominated by the idea of the transcendence of God (*CD*, II/1, 2). Brunner, too, has attacked liberal theology and has followed Barth in the revival of the doctrine of the divine transcendence (Brunner, *MW*).

IMMORTALITY

Religious liberalism considered the doctrine of the resurrection of the body grossly materialistic. In its eschatology it defended with vigor the doctrine of the immortality of the soul. In this regard it has been almost uniformly judged as Platonic. It agreed with Platonism that man had a lower, bodily self, and a higher, spiritual self. It agreed with Platonism that the body was a necessary evil, or at least a severe drag. It agreed with Platonism that the immortal part of man is the higher self, the personality, the soul.

Recent biblical theology has taken a drastically different line of thought. Studies in the Old and New Testament have shown that the biblical view of man concerns total man. Any biblical eschatology must take into serious account the total man. To assign immortality to a part of man is to go contrary to the biblical nature of man.

Oscar Cullmann has been very influential in pointing out the contrast between the Greek view of the immortality of the soul and the biblical view of the survival of the total man. He writes, for example, "The whole thought of the New Testament remains for us a book sealed with seven seals if we do not read behind every sentence there this other sentence: Death has already been overcome (death, be it noted, not the body); there is already a new creation (a new creation, be it noted, not an immortality which the soul has always possessed); the resurrection age is already inaugurated" (*ISRD*, p. 41). Brunner, too, has scored hard against the Platonic view of man and its great influence in Western thought (*D*, III, 383). The biblical doctrine of the resurrection means the survival of the total man — and that as a gift and work of grace, not in virtue of a natural immortality.

Although Barth has not as yet given us his eschatology, his great discussion of "Ending Time," with the penetrating discussion of death, would seem to place him in the camp of those who look for the survival of the total man (*CD*, III/2, 587ff., particularly p. 623, point 3). Speaking of the Christian hope, he says that the man of faith "is born again in His resurrection to a life in God concealed throughout the last time, and will be revealed in glory as one who has this life when Jesus returns in glory as the goal of the last time."

The articles on immortality in *BDT* and in *HCT* reflect this new emphasis in biblical theology.

INAUGURATED ESCHATOLOGY, *see* Eschatology

INAUTHENTIC EXISTENCE, *see* Authentic, Inauthentic Existence

INCARNATION

To Kierkegaard the supreme doctrine of Christianity is the incarnation. The union of God and man, it represents the maximum paradox that is so necessary for Kierkegaard's thought. Much of the contemporary revival of the doctrine of the incarnation stems from Kierkegaard.

Niebuhr, usually a close follower of Kierkegaard, deserts him at this point. Niebuhr believes that the incarnation is a symbolic truth. By "symbolic truth" he means a character event or fact that points beyond history and so becomes a source of disclosure of the eternal meaning of life and history (*NDM*, II, 61).

Niebuhr is very harsh with the Chalcedonian formulation, for in using metaphysical language for a symbolic truth it transmuted Christology into speculative reason. Taking his stance sharply against Chalcedon, Niebuhr writes that "all definitions of Christ which affirm both his divinity and humanity in the sense that they ascribe both finite and historically conditioned and eternal and unconditioned qualities to his nature must verge on logical nonsense" (*ibid.*, II, 61). Later on the same page he affirms that this doctrine does not merely verge on logical nonsense but *is* logical nonsense. When he returns to the subject (*ibid.*, pp. 70-71), he asserts that the historic doctrine of the incarnation is fraught with metaphysical absurdities and plain contradiction. But Niebuhr believes that formulations preserve in their unfortunate language the essence of the Christian faith that Jesus is morally and religiously divine.

In all of his dogmatic writings Barth has stood unequivocally for the deity of Christ and for a genuine incarnation. Speaking of Chalcedon he writes: ". . . the more exact determination of the relationship between God and man in the famous Chalcedon definition, which has become normative for all subsequent development in this dogma and dogmatics, is one which in our understanding has shown itself to be factually right and neces-

sary" (*CD*, IV/1, 133). In the same volume Barth describes
Jesus Christ as very God who became man for our redemption,
and his defense of the *filioque* clause makes sense only if he accepts the doctrine of the Trinity, the deity of Christ, and the
Incarnation (*ibid.*, I/2, 250).

Barth knows of the problem that Niebuhr raises. Can the
unconditioned and the conditioned be united in one person?
In discussing the freedom of God (*CD*, II/1, 314f.), Barth
raises the question and answers it this way. Man cannot know
of himself whether or not God can become incarnate (which
Niebuhr proposes to know). Only God knows this. The concrete answer is that God in His freedom did so will to limit
himself and become incarnate (see especially p. 315).

Brunner accepts the historic doctrine of the deity of Christ
and the incarnation (*D*, II, 350ff.). He writes: "The great,
unthinkable, unimaginable miracle of the Incarnation which the
Apostles proclaim is . . . that the Eternal Son of God, who from
all eternity was in the bosom of the Father, uncreated, Himself
proceeding from the Being of God Himself became Man; that
He, the eternal and personal Word of God, meets us in Jesus
Christ as man, of our flesh and blood, as our Lord, who in His
existence manifests to us the Being of His Father . . . Jesus IS
'by nature' God" (*ibid.*, II, 356). But Brunner is testy about
two matters. He does not like speculations about how the incarnation took place, and he consequently rejects the virgin
birth as speculation. He believes that Jesus Christ is true God
and true Man, but he does not approve of the explanation of
the incarnation in terms of natures.

Tillich believes that God is the ground of all being. Theologians find it difficult to see how from this premise Tillich can
defend the doctrines of the Trinity and incarnation as historically
understood. Tillich builds his Christology on the existential
assertion that Jesus is the Christ, and he attempts to make the
creeds of Nicea and Chalcedon say this. Thus he maintains
that he concurs with the creeds but only if the creeds concur
with his existential Christology. He says that the paradox of
Christianity is not the union of God and man, i.e., the historic
understanding of the incarnation: "the paradox of the Christian
message is that in *one* personal life essential manhood has ap-
peared under the conditions of existence without being con-
quered by them" (*ST*, II, 94). Tillich grants that one may speak
of God-manhood to emphasize the presence of the divine in the

manhood but it is better to speak of essential manhood. Thus the historic doctrine of the incarnation is replaced with an existential counterpart.

In his survey of modern debates in Christology, including the kenotic theories, G. C. Berkouwer maintains the position of Chalcedon but he does not believe that Chalcedon has said the last word on Christology (*PC*).

INCOGNITO

It was Kierkegaard's belief that if God became man there would not be anything unnatural or supernatural about this man. There would not be a direct knowledge that he was God incarnate. According to Kierkegaard a direct knowledge of God is paganism because in directness of knowledge no passion is excited. Therefore to protect inwardness and subjectivity and the possibility of genuine decision, Christ as God incarnate must appear as an ordinary man. Thus the incarnation was incognito. "The Teacher of our hypothesis was not immediately knowable; he could be known only when he himself gave the condition" (*PF*, p. 56).

The incarnation as God incognito is part of the Christology of both Brunner and Barth. Besides the notion of the incognito, Barth and Brunner add the notion that revelation in its human or worldly or earthly aspect must always appear as being within the course of ordinary events. Only by faith do we see the revelation that is present in the sign of revelation.

With reference to Christ this means that there was nothing special about Jesus Christ that would indicate that He was God manifest in the flesh. He must appear as a typical Jew among the other Jews of Palestine. Brunner says that clear disclosure of God in the incarnation would leave no room for faith (*TM*, p. 337). Therefore all communication in revelation must be indirect and therefore the incarnation as revelation must be incognito. The God of revelation (*Deus revelatus*) is also the God of veiling (*Deus velatus*). "His Deity is the secret of His Person, which as such does not enter into the sphere of history, at all" (*TM*, p. 343n).

Barth's structure of revelation in the incarnation is similar. Revelation is at the same time veiling and unveiling. God is *Deus revelatus* and *Deus absconditus*. Jesus appears before the men of His day simply as the Rabbi of Nazareth, i.e., incognito, and the humanity of Christ is not obviously revelation. "Manifestation is clearly not in itself or directly ascribed to His [human] existence as such" (*CD*, I, 371). "Thousands may have seen and heard the Rabbi of Nazareth. But this historical element was not revelation. Even the historical element at the resurrection of Christ, the empty grave regarded as an element in this event, that might possibly be fixed, was certainly not revelation. This historical element, like everything historical, is admittedly susceptible of an even highly trivial interpretation" (*ibid.*, p. 373).

Berkouwer notes the origin of the doctrine in Kierkegaard and its acceptance by Brunner and Barth, and he criticizes them on two points (*PC*, chap. 13). First, they build their view of the incognito on a false doctrine of revelation. Only if their view of indirect revelation is true is their doctrine of the incognito true. Second, they cannot adjust their theories to such an event as the transfiguration, where Christ's glory breaks out into the open. The real issue is not in the incognito but in sinful man's unwillingness to recognize revelation. The older Reformed theologians had their doctrine of incognito but it was not based upon a false theory of revelation. It was based upon the exegesis of Philippians 2:5ff.

INDIRECT COMMUNICATION

Kierkegaard taught that faith is decision, and that decision is real only if it is confronted with possibilities. If God communicates to us, He must so communicate as to keep the possibilities open and thus protect the reality of decision. Christianity therefore is an indirect existential communication. It is communication in that it does teach the incarnation; but to preserve the reality of the categories of decision and possibility it is an indirect communication. Stated in a different way, Christianity is not an obvious truth that compels a man to believe; it is not a truth whereby his sanity or integrity would be denied if he did not believe (cf. Reidar Thomte, *KPR*, pp. 192ff.).

Brunner also has a doctrine of indirect communication. Revelation comes to a man so that the self is not overpowered, and therefore it comes indirectly. God is veiled in His revelation. Christ, as God incarnate, did not throw men into panic when He approached them. They saw Him as a typical Jew of that day. Therefore the knowledge that He was God incarnate is indirect and known only through indirect communication. This keeps the gospel from being a piece of intellectualization and maintains the reality and possibility of human decision (cf. *BCR*, pp. 54-56).

INDIRECT REVELATION, *see* Revelation, Indirect

INSPIRATION

The revival of a strong doctrine of revelation in neo-orthodoxy has brought fresh interest in the inspiration of the Scriptures. If the Scriptures are in some sense a witness to revelation, they are in some sense inspired. Brunner has given much attention to the inspiration of the Scriptures, and he believes that modern physical science and historical science have broken down the edifice of the orthodox doctrine of inspiration (*RR*, p. 11).

Brunner never tires of making these two assertions: (1) the identification of the words of the Bible with the revelation itself is a major theological blunder; and (2) verbal inspiration is not only indefensible but it has been the cause of unspeakable harm in the Christian Church. The authority of the Bible and its inspiration is severely limited by Brunner. "In so far as the Bible speaks about subjects of secular knowledge, it has no teaching authority. Neither its astronomical, cosmological picture of the world, nor its geographical view, nor its zoological, ethnological or historical statements are binding upon us, whether they are in the Old Testament or in the New" (*D*, I, 48).

Furthermore, according to Brunner, the Scriptures do not themselves teach verbal inspiration nor their infallibility (*RR*, pp. 127-128). For all that the Bible is inspired. The entire writings of Paul and his activity are products of the guidance of the Holy Spirit. But this kind of inspiration of the Spirit does not rule out the human factors in the composition of Scripture (*ibid.*, p. 218). That which is inspired is the "bearer" of the word of God (*ibid.*, p. 129). Thus the authority and inspiration of the Bible is exactly at the point wherein it is a witness to the saving and revealing acts of God in Jesus Christ.

Barth is in agreement with Brunner that the Bible and revelation are not to be equated. Barth says an innumerable number of times that the Bible is a witness to revelation (*CD*, I/2). Barth agrees with Brunner that revelation is God's dynamic making Himself known; it is not a corpus of writings. Barth also believes that the historic doctrine of verbal inspiration and biblical infallibility has been broken down and may no longer be held. Such a view of the Bible as the older orthodox scholars held "materializes" revelation. Such a view represents the freezing of the relationship between revelation and Scripture (CD, I/1, 139).

Barth insists that making revelation personal and Christological does not lessen the verbal character of inspiration (CD, I/1, 157). Nevertheless, the verbal character of the Bible (which is necessary for the Bible to be an adequate witness) does not mean that God is encased in this verbal witness. God remains free and lord of the verbal character of Scripture (ibid.).

In discussing the meaning of II Timothy 3:16, Barth writes that to be inspired means to be "given and filled and ruled by the Spirit of God, and actively outbreathing and spreading abroad and making known the Spirit of God" (CD, I/2, 504). Here Barth takes inspiration to be the subjective disposition of the biblical writers and not the product of an action of the Holy Spirit. It is true that II Timothy 3:16 and II Peter 1:19-20 assign the production of the Scriptures to the Holy Spirit (ibid., p. 505), but this action by the Spirit did not exempt the writers from the vulnerability of their own errant personalities: "The men whom we hear as witnesses speak as fallible, erring men like ourselves" (ibid., p. 507).

In one passage Barth has put together clearly what he means by verbal inspiration. He speaks of the "verbalness" of inspiration. "If God speaks to man, He really speaks the language of this concrete human word of man. That is the right and necessary truth in the concept of verbal inspiration. If the word is not to be separated from the matter, if there is no such thing as verbal inspiration, the matter is not to be separated from the word, and there is real inspiration, the hearing of the Word of God, only in the form of verbal inspiration, the hearing of the Word of God only in the concrete form of the biblical word. Verbal inspiration does not mean the infallibility of the biblical word in its linguistic, historical and theological character as a human word. It means that the fallible and faulty human word is as such used by God and has to be received and heard in spite of its human fallibility" (ibid., pp. 532f.). For an investigation from a sympathetic yet critical viewpoint of Barth's views see K. Runia, *Karl Barth's Doctrine of Holy Scripture*.

B. B. Warfield has given the old orthodox view of inspiration its classic statement (*IAB*), and Carl Henry has given a stout defense of this view (*BDT*, pp. 286-289). The basic thesis is that the Bible in whole and in part is the word of God written (*ibid.*, p. 288). Inspiration does not mean the subjective state of the writers of Scripture but the production of inspired writings. No distinction can be made between the historical and doctrinal parts of Scripture because the doctrinal rests upon the historical (*ibid.*, 288). In a concluding paragraph Henry says that such a high view of inspiration does not lead to obscurantism in biblical criticism nor a glossing over of the evident problems of the Scriptural text.

For a composite and synoptic view of opinions of current scholars holding to the historic view of inspiration, see *RB*.

Bernard Ramm emphasizes that revelation is prior to inspiration, and that inspiration lives only from a strong doctrine of revelation. The function of inspiration is to provide the Church with a document of revelation in an authentic, trustworthy form (*RWG*).

INTELLECTUALIZATION

It was Kierkegaard's belief that Christianity existed only inwardly, subjectively, in the passion of faith. If the Christian faith is reduced to a set of doctrines that a man believes, then the Christian faith is intellectualized. We may define intellectualization as that view of faith which sees faith's action solely in the assent to doctrinal theses. In Roman Catholic theology "theological faith" is the acceptance of the *de Fide* teachings of the Church. This is a form of intellectualization. Insofar as the older Reformed and Lutheran theologians placed a supreme value on the acceptance of the truthfulness of historic confessions they were guilty of intellectualization. The evil in such intellectualization, according to Kierkegaard, is that there is no power of transformation of the self in the mere assent to doctrinal theses (cf. especially *CUP*). Faith is in the Teacher not in the teachings.

Brunner follows through on this theme very thoroughly when he attacks Greek intellectualism. "[Preaching] does not confront a person with a set of doctrines, with an idea to contemplate, a truth which is complete in itself, but it points man toward God who is already turning toward him. The word does not give itself to the intellect, but it places itself as a human organ at the disposal of the God who seeks to capture man for Himself. Here we are concerned with something fundamentally different from 'the knowledge of eternal truths'" (*RR*, p. 150).

Then Brunner explains that doctrines are necessary and that sound doctrine is a desirable thing. But the role of doctrine is purely instrumental. If we make doctrine an end, we intellectualize the faith; if we make doctrine the instrument of confrontation of God, then we keep it in the background where it belongs. Despising of doctrine leads to the mystical misunderstanding of the Christian faith (*ibid.*, p. 155). On the one hand, the personal character of the Word of God must never be lost; its "Thou" dimension as address must never be obscured. On the other hand, the address of God comes to us only in the form of doctrine. "The preaching of the Word which demands obedience can never take place without correct theological doctrine, nor without correct doctrinal ideas; but this is not sufficient" (*ibid.*, p. 154). The reason it is not sufficient is that God "Himself is the Word, and therefore can never be fully expressed in human words; no doctrinal formulation, however excellent, can claim to be the Word of God itself, or even the infallible 'correct' doctrine, which has been formulated and laid down once for all" (*ibid.*, p. 153).

Similar citations can be made from Barth's writings. Barth sees doctrines as *behests*. A behest is not something to be assented to as true, but something to be obeyed. The mere assent to a behest is intellectualization. He attacks the Roman Catholic doctrine of doctrine, and defends his own view that doctrines are commands, behests. The proper response to dogma is not assent but faith, obedience, decision. In fact, a behest is of such a character that its truth cannot be known apart from faithful obedience to it. (cf. *CD*, I/1, 309ff.).

The entire structure of Bultmann's thought is against intellectualization. Faith can only be in a possibility, and possibilities cannot be intellectually resolved or they would not be possibilities. They can be resolved only in decision. Thus he writes that "the incomprehensibility of God lies not in the sphere of theoretical thought but in the sphere of personal decision" (*JCM*, p. 43).

INWARDNESS

To emphasize the existential character of the Christian faith, Kierkegaard used a number of expressions such as inwardness, passion, subjectivity. Inwardness is the opposite of the objective attitude of the spectator. Kierkegaard often contrasts the external, objective, spectator, doctrinal approach to Christianity with the internal, passionate, and subjective appropriation: "Suppose that Christianity is subjectivity, an inner transformation, an actualization of inwardness, and that only two kinds of people can know anything about it: those who with an infinite passionate interest in an eternal happiness base this their happiness upon their relationship to Christianity, and those who with an opposite passion, but in passion reject it — the happy and the unhappy lovers" (*CUP*, p. 51). Later he writes, "suppose that someone wishes to communicate the following conviction: Truth is inwardness; there is no objective truth, but truth consists in personal appropriation" (*ibid.*, p. 71). He also equates proper existence with inwardness (*ibid.*, p. 216). He again writes that "to know a confession of faith by rote is paganism, because Christianity is inwardness" (*ibid.*, p. 201).

Kierkegaard says that the purpose of inwardness is to produce truth in action; to recognize truth in its deepest sense; to let truth permeate the whole being; to assume all the consequences of truth; to take truth with infinite seriousness. The reward of inwardness is certitude. The rational or intellectual proofs for God or for immortality do not produce certitude (*COD*, pp. 123-130).

Emil Brunner approaches Kierkegaard's doctrine of inwardness when he writes that "the doctrine of the Holy Spirit is the Christian answer to the truth in subjectivism, the doctrine of that inwardness which is not in the least degree our own" (*PR*, p. 113).

IRRATIONALISM

Irrationalism is the view that holds that truth or reality is known by means other than intellectual or rational. Hence non-rationalism is a more accurate term (cf. Ramm, "Irrationalism," *BDT*, p. 294). Kierkegaard and those theologians who follow him are charged with being irrationalists (see DeWolf, *RRR*).

There is a strong streak of irrationalism in Kierkegaard. He accepts the idea of the paradox, which he defines as "being the most improbable of things" (*PF*, p. 42). Furthermore, he repeatedly emphasizes the absurd, the leap, and the risk. Without

risk there is no faith and the greater the risk the greater the
faith (*CUP*, p. 188). The real truth is not known by the intellect
or reason, but by the non-rational way of inwardness and subjectivity. However Kierkegaard did leave it to reason to decide
when a man should decide against reason, in other words, reason
sets up the paradox.

Brunner follows Kierkegaard closely in his non-rationalism.
He has written the unusually strong statement that "God can
never be found along any way of thought; for indeed this idea
of God bursts through and destroys all the fundamental categories of thought; the absolutely antithetical character of the
basic logical principles of contradiction and identity. To want to
think this God for oneself would mean insanity" (*RR*, pp. 46f.).
Such a direct flouting of the basic laws of logic, the principles of
non-contradiction and identity, is almost without parallel in
theology.

Niebuhr also has an irrationalistic streak in his theology, but
from a different perspective. For example, he admits that the
doctrine of original sin is not acceptable to human reason. But
this does not mean the theologian must wilfully defy logic. On
the contrary, he is to follow logic as far as he can. But in the
use of logic we must recognize the complexity of the data, and
our logic might not yet be ready to handle this complexity.
"Loyalty to all the facts may require a provisional defiance of
logic, lest complexity in the facts of experience be denied for the
sake of a premature logical consistency" (*NDM*, I, 263). Niebuhr
has devoted an entire essay to this subject ("Coherence, Inco-
herence and Christian Faith," *CR*, pp. 175-203).

Tillich says that Christianity is paradoxical but not irrational
(*ST*, II, 90-91). There is irrationalism in man, but not in theology as such. The transition from essence to existence, from
the potential to the actual, from dreaming innocency to existential
guilt and tragedy, is irrational. It is pure act without rational
justification. However, the case is different in theology, where
we do not grant room for the absurd. But reason in theology
is not limited to technical reason, and therefore this reason must
reckon with the paradoxical and the dialectical.

Bultmann also has an element of the irrational in his thought.
Matters of fact can be settled by the reason but matters of existential destiny cannot. We cannot prove that faith should go
one way and not another. Faith is confronted with possibility

which it can resolve only by decision. Therefore faith is at heart and essence a non-rational act.

It is problematic to determine how much irrationalism there is in Barth's theology. Certainly Barth believes that God is rational. He writes: "In Him there is no paradox, no antinomy, no division, no inconsistency, not even the possibility of it" (*CD*, IV/1, 186). Concerning the Word of God he says that "the Word of God . . . is a rational and not an irrational event" (*ibid.*, I/1, 153). In his discussion of theology as a science he lists the criteria of science, which have a limited service to the theologian. He may take exception to them, but he must be aware of what he is doing when he does (*ibid.*, I/1, 8).

Barth admits that the coming of revelation to man involves a leap in that it is not the achievement of man's rationality but God's gift (*ibid.*, I/2, 234). But because it is a leap it is not irrational nor does it pledge us to an irrational theology. It is the very rational logic of revelation that there is such a leap. If theology were truly irrational at this point it would be very talkative and not let the leap be the leap (*ibid.*, p. 235). Furthermore, because the Word of God is spiritual and personal it is not thereby irrational (*ibid.*, I/1, 156). We are to follow logic as far as we can in theology, but we must never make a god out of logic. The unity in Christian theology is not the unity introduced by the law of non-contradiction but the unity of the person of Christ.

KAIROS, CHRONOS (*see also* Time)

Kairos (pl. *kairoi*) is one of the two Greek words for "time." It has been the subject of much comment in contemporary theology. Cullmann defines it in both its secular and theological meaning: "*Kairos* in secular usage is the moment in time which is especially favorable for an undertaking; it is the point of time of which one has long before spoken without knowing the actual date. . . . It is human considerations that cause a point of time to appear especially adapted for the execution of this or that plan, and thus make it a *kairos*. The New Testament usage with reference to redemptive history is the same. Here, however, it is not human deliberations but a divine decision that makes this or that date a *kairos*, a point of time that has a special place in the execution of God's plan of salvation" (*CT*, p. 39). Thus the history of redemption is made up of a series of *kairoi* (*ibid.*, p. 43).

John Marsh calls *chronos*, the other Greek word for time, time as chronologically considered and *kairos* as realistic time, i.e., the time of opportunity and fulfilment (*TWB*, p. 258). "The time of Jesus is *kairos* — and so is a time of opportunity" (*ibid.*, p. 262).

Tillich's use of *kairos* is more theological than lexical. He has summed up his views thus: "While chronos designates the continuous flux of time, kairos points out a significant moment of time" ("Kairos," *HCT*, p. 194). "Kairos points to unique movements in the temporal process, moments in which something unique can happen or be accomplished" (*ibid.*). The great central *kairos* of history was the appearance of Jesus as the Christ (*ibid.*, p. 195).

The word *kairos* can be used for unusual episodes in Church history. James Barr has reviewed these claims for *kairos* and *chronos*. He concludes that Cullmann and Marsh have not thoroughly checked out the lexical data and that their specialized interpretations of these words cannot be supported (*BWT*).

KERYGMA

The expressions "gospel" and "kerygma" are approximately the same. C. H. Dodd has made kerygma a common theological term. The kerygma which Dodd attempts to isolate is the message preached by the early church, and it is to be contrasted with teaching. This message is that the prophecies of the Old Testament are fulfilled and the new age has come with Christ; Christ was born of the seed of David; He died according to the Scriptures to deliver us out of this present evil age; He was buried; He rose the third day according to the Scriptures; He is exalted at the right hand of God as Son of God and Lord of the quick and the dead; He will come again as Judge and Saviour of men (*AP*, p. 17). The entire subject matter has been carefully restudied by R. Mounce (*ENNTP*). Barth has also expressed himself on the kerygmatic character of the ministry of Christ (*CD*, IV/2, 201ff.).

Bultmann has also spoken much of the kerygma. In speaking of the new understanding that man needs, Bultmann says that man cannot invent the terms of this new understanding. The terms are given in the kerygma. "When, therefore, the science

77

of New Testament seeks to present faith as the origin of the theological statements, it obviously must present the kerygma and the self-understanding opened up by it in which faith unfolds itself" (*TNT*, I, 239; cf. Ellwein, "Rudolph Bultmann's Interpretation of the Kerygma," *KH*, pp. 25-54).

KINGDOM OF GOD

The concept of the kingdom of God has been the subject of much research since the reversal of the liberal interpretation by Weiss and Schweitzer. According to religious liberals the kingdom of God is the ethical reign of God in human affairs. The Christians as a fellowship or brotherhood form a Church. As a society of men attempting to live up to the ethics of love, and to extend it into all human relationships, the Church is the kingdom of God (*IARL*).

Weiss and Schweitzer showed that the kingdom of God was a strong eschatological concept. Jesus expected the sudden, dramatic inbreaking of the kingdom within his lifetime. This eschatological perspective destroyed the liberal view of the kingdom and commenced a whole new series of investigations. G. Ladd says that in view of these investigations any idea of the kingdom of God must make peace with four kinds of statements: (1) the kingdom as a dynamic reign or rule (in contrast to the kingdom as a territory or area); (2) the kingdom as a future apocalyptic order which the righteous shall enter at the end of the age; (3) the kingdom as being in the midst of men; and (4) the kingdom as a present realm which men may enter ("Kingdom of God – Reign or Realm," *JBL*, 81:232-233, 1962; cf. Ladd, *CQ*).

The present attitude is that the New Testament teaching about the kingdom represents a tension between its current presence and its future reality. The kingdom is spoken of as having come, as having arrived, as being entered; it is also spoken of as coming in power and glory at the return of Christ. It is within this tension that we must think about the kingdom (*ENNTP*, pp. 30ff.; *TWB*, pp. 119-121; *HT*, pp. 197-201; *IDB*, III, 17-26).

C. H. Dodd has tried to end the tension with his realized eschatology. The so-called future eschatological period is in reality the now-period of the Christian Church. Eschatological truth is now in operation. Therefore the kingdom is here and keeps coming again and again. Others have accepted the premise that Jesus did expect the kingdom to come in a short period of time and that the early Church had that same expectation. In view of the delay of the kingdom's inbreaking it adjusted its theology accordingly and so must we.

Older nineteenth-century views have been carried over into the twentieth century by the conservatives. Amillennialism fosters the viewpoint that the kingdom of God is the spiritual rule of Christ in the Church. The final inbreaking of the kingdom corresponds with the beginning of the eternal state. The premillennialists stress both the present existence and the future earthly manifestation of the kingdom of God. Dispensationalists usually deny the existence of the kingdom of God now except in some dilute sense, but see it as occurring in the future, primarily as the fulfilment of Jewish hopes.

LANGUAGE, THEOLOGICAL, see Theological Language

LEAP (*see also* Risk)

Kierkegaard introduced the concept of the leap into theology. In discussing the proofs for the existence of God, he states that the proofs do not seem to prove anything as we work them out. But when we let go of them God suddenly exists! In that moment we have leaped (*PF*, pp. 33f.). Kierkegaard says that the leap belongs to the category of decision. Thus the leap may be towards sin as well as towards God (*COD*, pp. 42, 49; cf. *CUP*). Since faith is not the product of rational thought but a decision in the face of possibility, it is a leap.

Brunner states that "in the case of faith we cease to implant in the universal; here we can 'rely' on nothing, on neither universal facts nor grounds. Hence viewed from the standpoint of the 'natural man' faith is foolhardy, rashness, a leap in the dark. From the standpoint of faith itself, it is not rashness, but necessity; not a leap, but a case of being drawn and carried along" (*PR*, p. 29).

According to Bultmann that which faith believes is not provable nor verifiable by the usual canons of reason. Faith is confronted with existential possibility and makes a free decision. Because faith is therefore not the product of rational consideration, it is a leap.

Barth says that revelation becomes revelation to us by the

subjectivity granted by the Holy Spirit. It is not an achieve-ment of the human reason. Looked upon from the standpoint of logic, faith is not a motion from one logical point to the next logical point, but appears as a leap. On the one side are the signs of revelation; on the other side is the man who is aware of revelation. From the signs of revelation to the inward ex-perience of revelation there is only the leap. This is not irration-ality but grows out of the rational structure of revelation. In other words, the leap of faith is there in virtue of the fact that revelation is a pure gift of grace and in no sense a human achieve-ment (*CD*, I/2, 234f.).

LIBERALISM

Religious liberalism, liberalism, religious modernism, and modernism mean approximately the same thing. Liberalism refers more specifically to a spirit of inquiry to which nothing is sacrosanct. Modernism speaks more of the higher achievements of man in knowledge, especially critical and scientific, in the modern era. Religious liberalism is a product of modern philoso-phy, modern science, and modern enlightenment, which attempts to conserve the essence of Christianity in the modern or scientific or enlightened age. It strives to do this by a radical reinter-pretation of the Christian faith.

There were three movements of religious liberalism in the nineteenth century (see Macintosh, *TMT*). The first stems from German identity-philosophy or pantheism and is repre-sented by Schleiermacher. The second stems from the Kantian philosophy and is represented by Ritschl. The third stems from Hegelian philosophy and is represented by Biedermann.

The religious liberals agreed in applying without reservations the critical methods of literature, history, and sociology to the Scriptures. They generally accepted the uniformity of nature, the rejection of the supernatural, and the continuity of the human and the divine. They reinterpreted Christ not as God the Son incarnate in Jesus of Nazareth but as a specially and specifically divine filled man who perfectly reflected in terms of this earth the life of God in the soul.

Although K. Cauthen restricts his discussion of liberalism to the American scene, most of what he says can also be applied to British and continental liberalism. He distinguishes between two kinds of liberals: the evangelical liberals, who still attempt to keep Jesus Christ as the center of the Christian religion and its unique factor, and the modernistic liberals, who do not grant this place to Jesus even though at the end of their theology they might see unusual significance in Jesus. Cauthen finds three factors characteristic of liberalism.

(1) The principle of continuity erases the distinction between the supernatural and the natural. Speaking of this principle Cauthen writes: "There is practically no end to its application. It reduces the distinction between animals and men, men and God, nature and God, reason and revelation, Christ and other men, Christianity and other religions, nature and grace, the saved and the lost, justification and sanctification, Christianity and culture, the church and the world, the sacred and the secular, the individual and society, life here and hereafter, heaven and hell, the natural and the supernatural, the human and divine natures of Christ, etc." (*IARL*, p. 9).

(2) The principle of autonomy refers to the autonomy of human reason in religion and the autonomy of religious experience. The general result of this is to elevate experiences above theology; to reduce revelation from a divine self-disclosure to religious experience; and to make theology practical, and post-reflective of religious experience.

(3) The principle of dynamism teaches that the world is an open system. The world and man are in the process of making. Thus anything static in theology such as an infallible Bible or infallible truth or an infallible or at least fixed creed becomes suspect. Growth must be allowed for in the Bible, in theology, in man, and in social progress.

Neo-orthodox theology represents a vigorous protest against religious liberalism. Barth frequently attacks liberalism (*CD*, *passim*). The entire structure of Brunner's dogmatic thought is antithetic to liberalism. Tillich has written that "Neo-Protestantism is dead in Europe. All groups . . . consider that the last 200 years of Protestant theology are essentially erroneous. The year 1933 finished the period of theological liberalism stemming from Schleiermacher, Ritschl and Troeltsch" ("The Present Theological Situation in the Light of the Continental European Development," *TT*, 7:299, October 1949). Niebuhr calls liberalism an abortive effort to unite the biblical with the Graeco-Roman world-view (*NDM*, I, 5). It is naturalistic and optimistic, and in rejecting the rationally absurd fails to see the myth as revelation-bearing (*ibid.*, p. 145). The liberal notion of the evolving good could never show why its fulfilment was in Christ and not in some other man (*ibid.*, II, 54). Furthermore, "Liberal Protestantism belongs, on the whole, to the Renaissance rather than the Reformation side of the debate on human destiny" (*ibid.*, p. 158).

Replies and re-statements attempting to defend religious liberalism from the neo-orthodox attack have been made by some theologians (DeWolf, *CTLP;* Wiemen *et al.*, *RLR*).

LOVE

One of the most famous studies of the idea of love in the New Testament is Anders Nygren's *Agape and Eros.* Nygren states that the New Testament word for love, *agape,* and the Platonic word, *eros,* unfortunately became confused in patristic theology by Augustine's concept of *caritas.* Love in the New Testament is God's love in Jesus Christ, a love which is communicated only through Jesus Christ. It cannot be known from human experience, but must be known in the condescending of Christ in His earthly life and crucifixion. The Platonic notion of *eros,* on the other hand, refers to a longing of the soul for the world of ideas, and hence is basically an egocentric, desiring love (*HCT*, pp. 96-101). "*Eros* and *agape* signify two principally different orientations of life, two fundamental motives which compete with each other" (*ibid.*, p. 99).

The American theologian who has done the most with the theory of Nygren is Nels Ferré. Reviewing the future of an agape-theology, Ferré said that if Nygren's view of love could be freed from certain of its elements and applied fearlessly to every single Christian doctrine, a new day in theology might begin (*SC*, p. 241). Ferré has attempted to work out such a program by taking the concept of divine love as the synthesizing principle of theology. He writes that "the whole heart of the Christian faith is the endless and ultimately victorious love of God for which we are made and to which we are called. Nothing higher and nothing better can be imagined; if it could be, that, too, would be part of the central truth of the Christian faith: that the sovereign Lord is saving Love" (*SU*, p. 23).

Brunner sees the love for God as the material side of the image of God, in distinction from the formal side of the image, which is man's free responsibility before God. This freedom takes on material form as love for God. God as love is the very heart of the Christian gospel. The message that God is love is entirely new in the world. Brunner's development of the notion of love is much dependent upon Nygren (*D*, I, chap. 15). In an appendix on the history of the doctrine of love he notes to what extent both philosophy and theology are indebted to Nygren.

Barth's fundamental thesis in developing his doctrine of the divine attributes is that "God's being consists in the fact that He is the One who loves in freedom" (*CD* II/1, 322). He discusses the attributes of God under the aspects of the divine freedom and the divine loving. It is Barth's opinion that we do not move from human love to divine love by analogy, but rather that we only really understand love as we see it in the cross of Christ. Barth has a long note on *agape* and *eros* in which he sees *agape* as uniquely Christian, but he is not willing to consider *eros* as completely anti-Christian (*ibid.*, III/2, 279ff.).

Bultmann writes that when a man is freed from care for the world he is freed for love (*E*, p. 112). Being freed, man may live for others, which means to live for them in love. The believer is a new creature, and the fact that "his existence is an eschatological one, is made manifest by the fact that belief is effective in love" (*ibid.*).

MILLENNIUM, VIEWS OF

Premillennialism is the belief that Christ will return and set up a glorious earthly kingdom which will last a thousand years. This kingdom is the interim period between the return of Christ and the final judgment. It differs from amillennialism which sees the reign of Christ in the Church and therefore not demanding a visible reign, and from post-millennialism which sees a triumph of the Church in the preaching of the gospel through the supernatural agency of the Holy Spirit.

There are two species of premillennialism defended today. The more historic position is that the millennium is founded on the nature of the progress of the kingdom of God. Just as the Old Testament is preparatory for the Church period so the millennial period is preparatory for the eternal state. The kingdom of God is seen in its material and preparatory stage in the Old Testament; in its evangelistic and churchly aspect in the present period; in its public and glorious manifestation in the millennium;

and in its final triumph and form in the eternal state. (For a contemporary defense of this form of premillennialism, see Ladd, *CQ*.)

The second version is defended in the *Scofield Reference Bible* and in L. S. Chafer's *Systematic Theology*. According to this system David is promised a great kingdom as well as Abraham is promised a land. It was this national Jewish kingdom which John the Baptist and Jesus had in mind when they announced the coming of the kingdom. The Jews had the right notion of the kingdom but the wrong notion by which the kingdom would be established. Accordingly they rejected Jesus and with him the kingdom. The kingdom thus enters its mystery stage during the Church age. But God has not renounced his purpose to fulfil the land promises to Abraham and the kingdom promises to David. At the return of Christ these promises will then truly be fulfilled. National Israel will be restored; Christ will reign from Jerusalem; and all the nations of the world will be under his dominion.

MOMENT

The moment is a concept derived from Kierkegaard to describe the point at which a man responds with the passion of faith to the conditions which God grants for an encounter with him. To make this contact, God must appear as a Teacher, but to be a teacher, He must become man (*PF*, p. 18). According to Kierkegaard, eternity is not an extension of time in a linear relation, but a breakthrough into time in a perpendicular relation. This breakthrough is the moment, which is different from all other units of time in our lives. It is the moment of faith and paradox (*ibid.*, p. 50), the moment when we pass from Non-Being into Being (*ibid.*, p. 15).

Bultmann makes much use of the concept of moment in his essay on "The Crisis in Belief" (*E*, pp. 1-21). He contrasts the moment with a world-view, in which one has a general understanding of the relationship of things. But we are not related to God as if our knowledge of Him were like a world-view. Rather, God keeps confronting us in concrete decisions. These concrete confrontations are moments.

The concept of moment in Kierkegaard is very similar to the concept of encounter in neo-orthodoxy. Jewett finds a very similar doctrine of the moment in Brunner (*BCR*, p. 50).

MOTIF RESEARCH

Motif research is the methodology of the Swedish school of theologians. It is influenced by Kant, who claimed to have found the non-empirical elements in experience which gave the empirical elements their form. The Lundensian theologians claimed that Kant did not carry out this discovery in religion, and this is what they propose to do. The result is a scientific, non-normative, phenomenological approach to theology.

The goal of theology, according to this school, is to discover the fundamental ideas which compose the Christian faith. This methodology is called "motif research" (*motivforskning*). R. Johnson defines motif research as "a dispassionate, descriptive quest, pursued inductively, which is intended to lead beneath the surface, 'penetrate through the shifting forms,' and expose the controlling *grundmotiv*" (*APT*, p. 148, cf. Ferré, *SC*, chap. 2).

Aulén says that the purpose of theology is to make clear the meaning and significance of the Christian faith (*FCC*, p. 5). This clarification is a critical process. "By a critical analysis it must penetrate through shifting forms to the underlying and fundamental religious ideas and at the same time be continually mindful of that which is uniquely and essentially Christian" (*ibid.*, p. 6). Theology does not seek to prove these motifs to be true nor show them to be normative. The Christian faith is a given, a datum, and not the product of rational proof (*ibid.*).

In his various writings Nels Ferré has taken divine love as the fundamental motif of the Christian Scriptures and the Christian religion (cf. *APT*, p. 153).

MYTH (*see also* Demythologize)

The concept of myth does not have a uniform meaning in contemporary theology. The only way this concept can be treated is to note how different scholars use the term.

(1) *"Myth" used in a good sense.* Emil Brunner and Reinhold Niebuhr are theologians who believe that the Scriptures contain myths and that in a good sense. The basic reasoning of these men is that language about God must necessarily take the form of a myth. Statements about God are not factual statements such as scientists make, nor meaningless statements such as are found in pagan mythology. The biblical "myth" is the means of communication whereby a transcendent God makes known his will

to man. It is the means of expressing that which is historical and theological about man's existence.

Brunner has turned to the subject of myth several different times in his writings. According to him, the important element of the mythical in Christianity is that it keeps intact the historical character of Christianity, the decisive motion in the Christian gospel, and its personal character. If we remove the mythical from Christianity we make it non-historical and it becomes insipid abstract religion. But at the same time the biblical myth must not be confused with the pagan myth. According to Brunner there are four principal myths: Creation, the Fall, Reconciliation, and Redemption. The important matter in each of these myths is that they refer to the dividing line between time and eternity. He also characterizes the mythical as being super-historical, eschatological, remote from the sensuous but related to it, unique, and existential. In the final analysis it is a faltering way to state Christian truth, but it is the best way available (*TM*, pp. 277-396; *RR*, chap. 26; *D*, II, 268f.).

Niebuhr parallels Brunner's thought rather closely. He views a myth as the necessary mode by which the eternal God communicates with temporal man (*NDM*). Cullmann also uses the concept of myth approvingly. The beginning of time and the end of time are represented mythically in Scripture (*CT*, pp. 94f.).

(2) *"Myth" used in a bad sense, but acceptable.* Bultmann believes that the primitive kerygma was framed in Jewish and Greek myths (*KM*, pp. 1ff.). Bultmann apparently operates with two criteria for spotting the mythological. Positively, the mythological is any typical Greek gnostic redemptive myth or Jewish apocalyptic myth. Negatively, the mythical is that which runs contrary to the scientific understanding of the order of the universe. Bultmann does not believe that we are to accept the myth as such, but on the other hand he does not believe that we are to reject the myth outright. The myth contains the kerygma; therefore, we must penetrate through the myth and lay bare the original kerygma. Hence he proposes his famous demythologizing program to replace the total rejection of myth by nineteenth-century scholars, who properly spotted the mythological in the Christian Scriptures, but went too far in their rejection of it. By the help of existential philosophy we can strip off the myth and arrive at the original gospel.

(3) *"Myth" used in a bad sense and not acceptable.* Barth
defines myths as stories about the gods, and therefore not acceptable to Christian theology. He believes that there are myths
or fragments of myths in Scripture, but these myths do not per-
tain to the substance of the witness of Scripture to revelation.
For example he says that the Genesis account of creation is saga,
not myth. "The creation stories of the Bible are neither myths
nor fairy tales. This is not to deny that there are myths, and
perhaps fairy tales, in the materials of which they are constructed" (*CD*, III/1, 84). As far as Bultmann's entire demythologizing program is concerned, Barth has been a persistent
critic. He says, for example, that the entire first part of the fourth
volume of his *Church Dogmatics* is an intensive debate with
Bultmann (*CD*, IV/1, ix). For example, Bultmann flatly states,
regarding the resurrection that he does not believe in the en-
livenment of a corpse (*KM*, p. 8). Barth, to the contrary,
strongly defends the bodily resurrection of Christ.

NATURAL THEOLOGY (*see also* Revelation, General)

Many contemporary theologians make a distinction between
general revelation and natural theology. General revelation is
that which man may know of God in creation, providence, and
man. If this were reducible to knowledge of God it would be
called natural theology. Thus it is possible for a general revelation to exist without granting the existence of natural theology
on the grounds that human depravity prevents man from reduc-
ing general revelation to a knowledge of God.

Roman Catholic theologians and some Anglicans defend the
validity of a natural theology. Usually this is based upon the
general structure of the philosophy of Thomas Aquinas. It is
a teaching of the Roman Catholic Church that the existence
of God may be demonstrated by the human reason.

Brunner defends a position which he thinks is true to John
Calvin, namely, that there is a general revelation of God which
is valid, but which man cannot reduce to a natural theology
because he is a sinner (*RR*, p. 75; *D*, I, 132ff.; cf. David Cairns,
"Natural Theology," *HCT*, 249-255).

Barth, also claiming to follow Calvin, takes a more severe
position than Brunner. He does not believe in the distinction
between general revelation and natural theology. To Barth there

is neither natural theology nor general revelation. In at least a half-dozen major sections in the course of his *Church Dogmatics,* he flays the concept of natural theology (cf. II/1, 99ff.).

The entire issue is surveyed from the standpoint of historic Calvinism in G. C. Berkouwer's *General Revelation.*

NEO-EVANGELICALISM

Neo-evangelicalism is a movement among evangelicals that began in the mid-forties of the present century. Robert Lightner attributes the coining of the term to Dr. H. J. Ockenga (*NE,* p. 39). Once the fundamentalist-liberal battles subsided, and new currents began to flow in contemporary theology, differences within the conservative, orthodox, evangelical camp began to appear. Three significant events marked the emergence of neo-evangelicalism. The first was the founding of Fuller Theological Seminary with the avowed intention of defending orthodoxy on the highest academic plane possible. The second was the world-wide evangelistic campaigns of Billy Graham, which called for inter-church cooperation. The third was the founding of the journal *Christianity Today.*

The neo-evangelical agrees with the fundamentalist in that he affirms a strong, historic Christian confession, but he disagrees in matters of emphasis and strategy. Ockenga originally criticized fundamentalism for having wrong attitudes, wrong strategies, and wrong results. But, as Lightner points out, there are more issues than these. The differences seem to center on two problems. The neo-evangelical feels that fundamentalism elevates secondary and tertiary doctrines to the rôle of cardinal ones; and secondly, the fundamentalist does not work with the right theological materials, either historic or contemporary. Both C. F. H. Henry and E. J. Carnell attempt to strengthen their positions by disassociating themselves from fundamentalism (Henry, *ER*; Carnell, *COT*). The fundamentalist rejoinder is that neo-evangelicalism is a dilution or compromise of the faith which seriously weakens the Christian position.

NEO-LIBERALISM

The term neo-liberalism is used in two different ways in recent theology. According to some orthodox theologians, neo-orthodoxy is merely old liberalism in a new form. The apparent novelty in neo-orthodoxy is deceptive, it is claimed, for if one looks at the original presuppositions, particularly that of the autonomy of man, or Kantianism, the neo-orthodox retains the liberal stance. Hence, it is not neo-orthodoxy as much as it is neo-liberalism (cf. Van Til, *NM*).

The term neo-liberalism is also used of Bultmann. He is accused of repeating the pattern of liberalism in the existentialist mood in contrast to the older idealistic mood. (1) He carries on with the historico-critical methodology much in the same spirit as the older liberals; (2) he has an essentially anthropocentric theology, for no statement about God is allowed to stand if it cannot be translated into existential terms for man; and (3) he grants the priority of a philosophy over exegesis, in that existentialism forms the pre-understanding for the interpretation of the New Testament.

NEO-ORTHODOXY

The theological movement spearheaded by Barth and Brunner has been called Crisis Theology and Dialectical Theology, but the most commonly used name for it is neo-orthodoxy. The story of its origin, its founders, and their eventual separation into divergent movements has been told by Henri Bouillard (*KB*, I). Neo-orthodoxy represents a spectrum of beliefs or positions. In some instances a neo-orthodox theologian is but an orthodox theologian with a neo-orthodox corrective, and in another instance it is a liberal theologian with a neo-orthodox corrective. The following eleven points attempt to state in general the nexus of beliefs forming neo-orthodox thought.

(1) Neo-orthodox theologians believe that they are the true heirs of the Reformation. What is called "orthodoxy" is really a formalized, rationalized, and crystallized version of the Reformers. But the dynamism of the Reformers has been lost. Neo-orthodoxy claims that it reclaims the original dynamism of the theology of the Reformation. Hence there is considerable citation of Luther and Calvin in neo-orthodox literature. W. Hordern thus entitles his defense of neo-orthodoxy as *The Case for a New Reformation Theology.*

(2) Neo-orthodox theologians believe that orthodoxy, Roman Catholicism, and liberalism represent dead ends as options in theology. Roman Catholic theology is corrupted by its doctrine of Tradition and by its view of dogmas as eternally settled truths of revelation. Orthodoxy defaults in that it has a similar view

of dogma as that of Roman Catholicism, accepts a doctrinaire view of revelation, and defends a view of the inspiration of the Bible which is out of keeping with critical biblical knowledge. Liberalism in stressing the autonomy of man loses the magisterial Word of God and therefore makes theology impossible.

(3) Neo-orthodox theologians believe that the Bible is not revelation itself but is a witness to revelation. The Word is not the same as the words, even though the Word is found only through the instrumentality of the words. Orthodoxy is wrong in identifying the words of the Bible with the words of God, and in identifying revelation with the words of the Bible. Liberalism is wrong in that it identified revelation with the best in man (the best being divergently interpreted), and therefore lost the theological significance of the Bible. Religious certainty is not to be found in orthodoxy's inerrant Bible, nor in the self-authenticating religious experiences of religious liberalism, but in the confrontation of man by the Word of God in Jesus Christ through the power of the Holy Spirit.

(4) Neo-orthodox theologians believe that revelation is a dynamic concept, God Himself in act, man in confrontation with Jesus Christ, the disclosing activity of the Holy Spirit. Revelation is not in words — not even the biblical words — nor in documents, but is God's encountering of man again and again and again. Revelation is address, speech, meeting, confrontation, dialogue. Preaching, the Scriptures, and sacraments are witnesses that revelation has occurred and promises that it will occur again.

(5) Neo-orthodox theologians believe that special events of Scripture have a special character. These special events cluster around creation, redemption in Christ, and the end-times. Brunner and Niebuhr prefer to use the word *myth* in this connection, whereas Barth prefers the term *saga*. Such terms indicate that the realities they signify are true historical realities, but historical in a very special sort of way.

(6) Neo-orthodox theologians believe that existentialist philosophy is the best point of departure for Christian theology. Brunner and Niebuhr both confess their indebtedness to Kierkegaard. Barth admitted earlier influence by existentialism but later attempted to purge his system of existentialism. However, two things may be noted. First, the Swedish theologians who are close to the analytic school of philosophy classify Barth

among the existentialist theologians. Secondly, Barth persists in using some existential lumber in his theological construction.

(7) Neo-orthodox theologians believe that the key doctrines of theology are in the logical form of a paradox. Brunner is the nearest heir to Kierkegaard at this point. Niebuhr also believes in paradoxes, but on the grounds that any attempt to remove the paradox results in a premature rationalization of theology. Barth believes that logic and consistency should be followed as far as they can be, but the theologian must never make a god out of the law of contradiction or any other law of logic. God as transcendent is always escaping human conceptual schemes.

(8) Neo-orthodox theologians believe in the absolute centrality of Jesus Christ. This is particularly true of Barth and Brunner who see in Christ the God-Man of the ancient confessions of the Church. Although Niebuhr does not come this far he nonetheless sees in Jesus Christ the central figure of Christian redemption and revelation.

(9) Neo-orthodox theologians believe in the real sinfulness of man. The conceptions of original righteousness, original sin, Adam, and the Fall are given reinterpretations, but much that the older orthodox doctrines signified is retained. These doctrines are restated not as historical events or conditions which once prevailed, but as the historical conditions under which all men exist. They are the kinds of things which continuously repeat themselves. Orthodoxy was right in seeing the tragic proportions of sin, but wrong in taking Genesis 3 so historically literal. Liberalism erred by seeing nothing in Genesis 3 but a Hebrew explanation as to why man had to work so hard, sex was shameful, and snakes crawled on their bellies.

(10) Neo-orthodox theologians generally agree that God is transcendent. The theologian who recovered and properly stated the divine transcendence was Kierkegaard. Liberalism was too much influenced by idealistic philosophy to catch the spirit of the biblical doctrine of the transcendence of God. But the biblical and Kierkegaardian doctrine of transcendence is recaptured in neo-orthodoxy. This means that there are sharp boundaries between God and man, heaven and 'earth, and time and eternity.

(11) Neo-orthodox theologians generally agree that any rationalistic or empirical approach to God is wrong, if not wicked. Natural theology, theistic proofs, and Christian evidences are all rejected as false approaches to God. In agreement with Calvin

and Luther in Reformation times, and Kierkegaard in recent times, they claim that the experience of the gospel is itself self-validating.

NEW BEING

New Being, as the term is used in the theology of Paul Tillich, is primarily an existential term, corresponding to the existential sense of the German word *Sein*. When Tillich uses the term "being," he does not mean it in the traditional ontological sense of the English word "being." "Old Being," for Tillich, is life in sin, the inauthentic life. New Being is brought in by Jesus as the Christ; hence, in Tillich's vocabulary, New Being stands for redemption and salvation. Because Jesus as the Christ brought New Being, all men may now have New Being. According to Tillich, the biblical term that is closest to New Being is "new creation" (*ST*, I, 49).

Applied personally, New Being is a term of creativity, regeneration, and eschatology (*ibid.*, I, 55). It means reconciliation and reunion with God, the entrance of new meaning and new hope, representing the undoing of the demonic. It is not, however, restricted to Christ and the believers, but may be applied to society and to the universe (*ibid.*, I, 49).

OBJECTIVE CHRISTIANITY

It was Kierkegaard's conviction that Christianity existed only in subjectivity and therefore did not exist in objectivity. "He who has an objective Christianity and none other, is *eo ipso* a pagan, for Christianity is precisely an affair of spirit, and so of subjectivity, and so of inwardness" (*CUP*, p. 42). If Christianity were objective it could be proved and tested by ordinary rational means. This would mean that a person could be completely objective and detached from Christianity and yet prove it to be true. But Christianity exists only in subjectivity. It is the communication of a passion in inwardness and subjectivity, and this is the locus of its confirmation.

A similar strain is to be found in Bultmann. Bultmann removes all the acts of God and the decisions of faith from the category of the objectively verifiable. To the degree that he does this, he concurs with Kierkegaard's thesis that objective Christianity does not exist.

ORIGINAL RIGHTEOUSNESS

Niebuhr's discussion of original righteousness is found in *NDM* I, chapter 10, *"Justitia Originalis."* He makes it clear that he does not interpret the story of Adam literally, but rather takes it as a myth. Original righteousness is not something which Adam had and lost. It is something which all men have. Niebuhr uses the analogy of health. If a sick man did not have a measure of health, he would be dead. Therefore, even in his sickness he can contemplate his health. Correspondingly, the sinner in his sin can yet retain something of original righteousness. Man has some knowledge of what he ought to be. In his own historical existence he yet transcends his existence and becomes aware of a law to which he ought to conform. This law to which he ought to conform is original righteousness. No man is so depraved as not to have fleeting feelings of a higher or better standard to which he owes allegiance. Having established the formal character of original righteousness as the law by which we recognize something that is higher than our behavior, Niebuhr then asks what is the concrete character of this law. His answer is the law of love — love to God and love to neighbor. The original righteousness of which we concretely come short is the law of love.

Brunner does not discuss the subject as such, but in its place he discusses the *imago Dei*. The formal image of God is man's freedom in responsibility and the material image is man's love to God and neighbor. Original righteousness would then be found in a man who by his freedom and responsibility loved God and his neighbor.

Barth, like Brunner, does not discuss the concept as such. If there is anything in Barth that is similar to the concept of original righteousness, it is at two points. Barth speaks of the real man in contrast to the phenomenal. The whole man, the real man before God, would then functionally have original righteousness in Barth's view. Secondly, Barth speaks much of Jesus Christ as the man for God. The perfect humanity of Jesus Christ is then analogically the functional equivalent of original righteousness with Barth.

Tillich discusses this topic under the goodness of man at creation (*ST*, I, 259). According to him the notion of Adam as a perfect and remarkable man makes the Fall unintelligible. It makes more sense, says Tillich, if we think of man originally in a state of dreaming innocency, a stage of infancy before contest and decision. "The goodness of man's created nature is that he is given the possibility and necessity of actualizing himself and of becoming independent of his self-actualization, in spite of the estrangement unavoidably connected with it" (*ibid.*).

OTHER, WHOLLY (*see also Deus Absconditus*)

The concept of the Wholly Other is derived from Kierkegaard's doctrine of divine transcendence. This is expressed in the infinite qualitative difference between God and man. In a turgid paragraph in *PF*, Kierkegaard speaks of the Unknown. The meaning seems to be that reason meets God as the Unknown. God is the Unknown because the Unknown "is different, the absolutely different" from the human reason (*ibid.*, p. 35). The reason cannot go against its own principles, so it has no way of mastering the Unknown.

A similar concept appears in Brunner. "As the Wholly Other, God is the Holy One, the Incomparable, the Unique. As the Wholly Other, He can never be fully understood by any creature" (*RR*). And further: "He alone is mysterious who comes to us from a region beyond *all* spheres known to us, who breaks through the barriers of our own experience of the world and the self, and enters into our world, as one who does not belong to it" (*D*, I, 118).

Niebuhr defines "The Other" as the One who meets us "at the limit of our consciousness," and in being The Other is not known to us except through specific revelations (*NDM*, I, 130).

Barth has a similar concept in his doctrine of the hiddenness and incomprehensibility of God which he develops extensively (*CD*, II/1, 179ff.). In passing he remarks that "between God and man as between God and the creature in general, there consists an irrevocable otherness" (*ibid.*, p. 189).

PARADOX

Hegel's logic was a logic of three terms. A thesis is postulated which suggests its opposite, the antithesis. Since the mind cannot rest in the tension of the thesis and the antithesis, it must mediate or reconcile this tension. This is done by the introduction of the third step, the synthesis. Thus Being suggests

Non-Being, and these two terms are reconciled in Becoming (cf. Ramm, "Dialectic," in *BDT*, pp. 165f.).

Kierkegaard reduced the three terms of Hegel into the two terms of a paradox. Man as an existent cannot see things from the perspective of eternity. He can only see things as finite man and therefore as paradoxical. Certainly there are no paradoxes for God. For example, Kierkegaard wrote that "the eternal essential truth is by no means itself a paradox" (*CUP*, p. 183). But man as existent is prevented from making any system. He cannot reconcile the tensions in the logic of existence. Existential truth can appear to him only as paradoxical.

But there is more to this than man's existential limitations. The paradox carries an existential charge of energy. The paradox which stuns the intellect at the same time excites the passions. For example, he wrote: "However one should not think slightingly of the paradoxical; for the paradox is the source of the thinker's passion, and the thinker without a paradox is like a lover without a feeling" (*PF*, p. 29).

Kierkegaard locates the Absolute Paradox in Jesus Christ as a single man who happens to be God-incarnate. This is bringing together the polar opposites and therefore constitutes the maximum stunning of the intellect. For example, he wrote "that God has existed in human form, has been born, grown up, and so forth, is surely the paradox *sensu strictissimo*, the absolute paradox" (*CUP*, p. 194). This work is filled with references to the paradox because the paradox is the logical form of truth that in the meantime is exciting passion, inwardness, and faith.

Kierkegaard did not wallow in the paradoxical. The paradoxical pertains to existential truth and not to the sciences and general learning. Furthermore, it was the mind which led the mind to the point where it must go against itself. Not just any tension will do. The horns of the paradox must be established by the vigorous application of the intellect.

Brunner and Niebuhr both reflect Kierkegaard's conviction that the mark of existential truth is the paradoxical. Brunner writes that "the object of faith is something which is absurd to reason, i.e., paradox; the hall-mark of logical inconsistency clings to all genuine pronouncements of faith" (*PR*, p. 55). In *RR* he does not give a great deal of attention to the paradoxical, but the same idea appears in the manner in which he stresses the discontinuity between revelation and the rational systems of man. The paradoxical is not merely a logical difficulty which makes theology difficult but it inheres in the very nature of the Christian faith.

Niebuhr's position is milder. His basic stance in all matters of rationality is that the complexity of the data forbid premature systematization. In our present finite condition we cannot help but face the paradoxical (*NDM*, I, 25). Such examples of the paradoxical are man being a creature yet a child of God (*ibid.*, p. 25); that man's activities in history are constructive yet destructive (*ibid.*, p. 38); that man can save his life only by losing it (*ibid.*, p. 77); or that man is a finite creature of nature yet transcends nature (*ibid.*, p. 120).

Tillich believes in the paradoxical, but takes another approach. He disagrees with Brunner that the paradoxical represents the inevitable clash of reason with faith so that the paradoxical is that which offends rationality. Tillich does not believe that the paradoxical offends rationality. Rather, the paradoxical means that God transcends human expectations. "Paradoxical means 'against the opinion,' namely the opinion of finite reason. Paradox points to the fact that in God's acting finite reason is superseded but not annihilated; it expresses the fact in terms which are not logically contradictory but which are supposed to point beyond the realm in which finite reason is applicable" (*ST*, I, 57).

In another definition of the paradox Tillich writes that "the logical form in which the perfectly concrete and the perfectly absolute are united is the paradox. All biblical and ecclesiastical assertions about the final revelation have a paradoxical character. They transcend ordinary opinion, not only preliminarily but definitively; they cannot be expressed in terms of the structure of reason but must be expressed in terms of the depth of reason. If they are expressed in ordinary terms, logical contradictory statements appear. But these contradictions are not the paradox, and no one is asked to 'swallow' them as contradictions. . . . The paradox is the reality to which the contradicting form points; it is the surprising, miraculous, and ecstatic way in which that which is the mystery of being universal is manifest in time, space, and under the conditions of existence, in complete historical concreteness" (*ibid.*, I, 150f.).

It is difficult to determine the role of the paradoxical in Barth. He does state that the incarnation is not a blind paradox (*CD*, IV/1, 12). He also affirms that there is no paradox in God (*ibid.*, p. 186). He cautions repeatedly against theological irrationalism. But on the other side of the ledger are his frequent claims that man has no means of testing the revelation of God. It is given with the authority and power of God apart from all human schemes and testings. Thus he makes the claim that the Word of God can establish itself in man's rationality. But just how this given datum of the Word which is so unexpected and so contrary to human religious notions strikes the human mind in its logical form Barth does not spell out.

PASSION

Passion is one of the more central concepts of Kierkegaard. He takes Aristotle's list of passions and tops it with faith. In so doing Kierkegaard breaks with a great tradition in Western philosophy which came to a climax in Hegel, namely, that what is deepest in man is reason. Kierkegaard affirms that the deepest in man is passion.

Kierkegaard makes many references to passion. In an absolutely perfect world there would be no faith and no passion (*CUP*, p. 30). Passion is "infinite personal interestedness" (*ibid.*). Philosophy teaches the way of objectivity but Christianity teaches the way of subjectivity. Subjectivity is the person in the state of truth. To be a person in truth is to intensify passion to its highest pitch and this passion is the same as subjectivity (*ibid.*, p. 117).

In another passage he says that modern philosophy holds passion in contempt (*ibid.*, p. 176). But "passion is the culmination of existence for an existing individual" (*ibid.*). "Inwardness in an existing subject culminates in passion; corresponding to passion in the subject the truth becomes a paradox; and the fact that the truth becomes a paradox is rooted precisely in its having a relationship to an existing subject" (*ibid.*, p. 177). Continuing on another page, he says that "all existential problems are passionate problems, for when existence is interpenetrated with reflection it generates passion. To think about existential problems in such a way as to leave out the passion, is tantamount to not thinking about them at all, since it is to forget the point, which is the thinker is himself an existing individual" (*ibid.*, p. 313).

PERPENDICULAR

Barth's doctrine of revelation is that it is given by God's freedom, grace, and sovereignty. Thus he speaks of it coming per-

pendicularly from above — *senkrecht von oben*. He also speaks
of revelation taking place "vertically from heaven" (*CD*,
I/1, 379).

PERSONALISM

Personalism is the belief that the human self is a metaphysical
reality and a clue to the structure or meaning of the total cosmos.
We may distinguish two kinds of personalism. There is the
idealistic personalism in the tradition of Bowne, Brightman, and
Flewelling. Taking the concept of person as a fundamental
category, it sees the universe as God and a society of persons.
It finds itself a ready ally to religious modernism in the domain
of theology. It is still of some importance in that it is a personalism carried on by those influenced by Brightman in particular
(cf. *EOR*, p. 576; *TCERK*, II, 867f.).

The second kind of personalism is existential personalism. It
has its roots in Kierkegaard, Ebner, and Brunner. Kierkegaard's
anthropology is the anthropology of the human person conceived
as an existent whose chief task in life is to decipher what it
means to exist. This existence is focused upon eternal happiness,
and about this eternal happiness we should be infinitely, personally, and passionately concerned (*CUP*, p. 23). The mark of
the person concerned with existence is that he is infinitely,
personally, and passionately concerned. Thus one can summarize Kierkegaard's position by stating that he was concerned with
discovering the possibilities of existence for man conceived as a
person whose duty it is to exist authentically.

Martin Buber's *I* and *Thou* represent another form of existential personalism (*IAT*). In this little volume an intimate, mystical, existential personalism is developed. The most fundamental
relations of life are the person-person relationship which Buber
indicates by the expression "I-Thou," and the Person-person relationship (of God to man) indicated by "Thou-I."

In contrast to F. J. McConnell, who developed a theology of
religious liberalism around the personalistic idealism of his day,
Brunner develops a neo-orthodox theology relying heavily upon
the personalism of Kierkegaard, Ebner, and Buber (cf. *BCR*,
pp. 67-82). It can also be said that the anthropology of Niebuhr
and Tillich is basically that of existential personalism because of
their indebtedness to the existential tradition. The "nature" of
man in Niebuhr's *NDM* is certainly that of the existential per-

sonalist. Barth has a great admiration for Buber and frequently uses his terminology. It cannot then be denied that there is a measure of existential personalism in the theology of Barth.

POINT OF CONTACT

One of the more important questions of the twentieth-century theology is whether or not there is in the sinner a point of contact (German, *Anknüpfungspunkt*) for the gospel. If man is a sinner, and if thereby he reckons the word of the cross to be foolishness, how is it possible for him ever to consider it to be the wisdom of God. To what do we appeal?

According to Barth, Brunner had argued in his book, *Gott und Mensch* (1930), that the humanity and personality left over from the Fall formed the connecting point of the Word of God with man (*CD*, I, 273). However, Brunner postulates a somewhat different theory when he says that the point of contact is the sense of guilt (*RR*, p. 215). In an interesting footnote he writes: "Hence the 'bad' conscience, the sense of guilt, is the point of contact for all the preaching of the gospel" (*ibid.*, p. 302n).

Barth takes a more radical view. He believes that sin so destroys the image of God in man that there is no point of contact (*CD*, I/1, 273). The point of contact is the point of contact which the Word of God itself makes in man. The Word of God creates faith, and it is this Word-created faith which is the point of contact. Thus Barth writes: "This point of contact is, therefore, not real outside faith but only in faith. In faith a man is created by the Word of God for the Word of God, existing in the Word of God, not in himself, not in virtue of his humanity and personality, nor from the standpoint of creation, for what is possible from the standpoint of creation from man to God has actually been lost through the fall" (*ibid.*).

The issue of point of contact is also relevant in apologetics. Roman Catholic theologians believe that in the philosophy of Aristotle there is a point of contact with unregenerate men. Brunner believes in conversation at least to the point of debating, for he calls his apologetics "eristics" (*q.v.*). Barth's position seems to be that the best "defense" of the Christian faith is a fully explicated dogmatics. Or more tersely, "my dogmatics is my apologetics." Some theologians in the Reformed tradition find a partial point of contact in the doctrine of common grace.

Bultmann writes an essay concerned with the subject of point of contact ("Points of Contact and Conflict," *E*, chap. 7). Bultmann's thesis is that the Word of God comes to man as both conflict and contact. In the sense that it comes as conflict, as judgment upon man and his religion, there is no contact. There is nothing of the Word of God in man that responds to and corresponds to the Word of God which comes to him in Christian preaching. But conflict means relationship and therefore there must be a point of contact or there could be no conflict. Bultmann finds three kinds of contact. (1) Man does carry with him the question of his existence. Even though his answer is wrong and his state of being is sinful he yet carries this question. And it is these wrong answers that the Word of God conflicts with, and so man's sinfulness is itself the point of contact. (*ibid.*, p. 137). (2) Human preaching has to be in a man's own language, and this means also in the relevancy of man's ideas of God, religion, man, and ethics. This is the second point of contact. (3) Bultmann enlarges on this second point by showing how Paul used for Christian purposes popular Hellenistic philosophy, Hellenistic mystery religions, and Gnosticism. But Paul kept the Christian content and the conflict clear even though he used these concepts.

POINTER

Orthodox theology has maintained that the Scriptures themselves are the word of God written and therefore are directly revelational. Neo-orthodox theologians have redefined revelation in such a way that it is impossible to call Scripture directly the revealed word of God. Revelation is dynamically redefined. It is God acting and speaking, to which acting and speaking man responds in faith and obedience. It is only in the dynamism of the divine speaking and the human obeying that one can speak of revelation.

In that this event is completely personal, a God-man relationship, its existence is known only indirectly. It can only be pointed to. Thus surrounding revelation, indicating its existence and its nature, are a number of pointers. The doctrines of the Bible are such pointers, and in this sense they are a form of revelation. Thus Brunner says that the doctrinal message of the Bible is a pointer towards the supreme Truth (*RR*, p. 152). He also writes that "doctrine is only a pointer, even though it may be a clear and useful pointer" (*ibid.*, p. 156).

Barth's position is virtually the same. Revelation is not a book nor a doctrine but something which occurs. We know that it occurs in virtue of pointers. Barth speaks of pointers (*CD*, I/1, 57, 65), signs, and witnesses. He has three rather long discussions of the signs of revelation (*ibid.*, I/, 223ff., 457ff., 500ff.). The Bible is the chief sign of revelation. But the word which occurs most frequently in I/2 is witness. The Bible is the witness to revelation but not the revelation itself. It is the recollection that revelation has occurred and the promise that it will occur again.

PRE-UNDERSTANDING

Bultman believes that any subject matter must be approached with a certain set of presuppositions corresponding to the nature of the subject matter. "Without a pre-understanding no one can ever understand what is said anywhere in literature about love or friendship, or life and death — or, in short, about man generally" (*EF*, p. 64). Thus history, literature, and music each has its pre-understanding without which nothing could be learned of these subjects. However, this is not an arbitrary matter but is determined by the character of the subject matter.

There is also a pre-understanding to religion, and if to religion, to Christian faith. Since religion and the Christian kerygma deal with the fundamental problem of the meaning and existence of the self, we turn to existential philosophy for our pre-understanding. Existential philosophy does not give us the answers, and is no substitute for the kerygma. But it does give us the pre-understanding whereby we are able to make sense out of the New Testament. Important at this point is the essay by Bultmann on "Is Exegesis without Presuppositions Possible?" (*EF*) and the chapter on "Modern Biblical Interpretation and Existential Philosophy" (*JCM*).

PRIMAL HISTORY

Primal history is a term which has had some usage by neo-orthodox writers. The term, first used by Overbeck, was used by Barth in his earlier writings but he has since abandoned it in favor of such expressions as "pre-history," "saga," and "legend." Brunner uses the term to refer to creation, original righteousness, the Fall, and original sin (*D*, I, 17). He writes: "It is only from the standpoint of . . . primordial history that the general character of history can be known at all. [Primal history] is the germ of all history; what the historian relates to us as 'history' is its manifestation in space and time" (*PR*, p. 123).

Primal history consists of those factors in history (not events as such) which characterize man's historical existence. It is not in history in the sense that scientific historiography can cope with it, yet it is in history in that it determines the character of man's historical existence.

PROOFS FOR THE EXISTENCE OF GOD, see Theistic Proofs

PROPITIATION, see Expiation

REALISM

Realism is used in contemporary theology to indicate a fresh assessment of the doctrine of sin. It stands in contrast to the proposed optimism in the assessment of sin in religious liberalism. Yet realism is not a return to the orthodox doctrine of Adam, the Fall, and universal depravity through the Fall. W. M. Horton in a provisional definition of realism defines it as follows: "The word 'realism' suggests to me, above all, a resolute determination to face all the facts of life candidly, beginning preferably with the most stubborn, perplexing and disheartening ones, so that any lingering romantic illusions may be dispelled at the start; and then, *through* these stubborn facts and not *in spite* of them, to pierce as deep as one may into the solid structure of objective reality, until one finds whatever ground of courage, hope, and faith is *actually* there, independent of human preferences and desires, and so casts anchor in that ground" (*RT*, p. 38). Mary Frances Thelen has written *Man as Sinner in Contemporary American Realistic Theology* to document the revival of sober views of human sin and depravity as found in recent theology. The leader in this movement is Reinhold Niebuhr.

Thus, broadly understood, Brunner (who significantly influenced Niebuhr) and Barth belong to the new realistic appraisal of sin (cf. Brunner, *MIR; D*, II, chap. 3; Barth, *CD*, IV/1, § 60).

REALISM, BIBLICAL, see Biblical Realism

REALIZED ESCHATOLOGY, see Eschatology

RELIGION

The status of religion and non-Christian religions has been discussed in contemporary theology; by Emil Brunner, for example (*RR*, chaps. 15-17). Brunner's basic thesis is that Christianity is the one true religion of God in that it is an absolute revelation. One may be tolerant of other peoples and their religions while holding to the absolute character of the Christian revelation (*ibid.*, p. 219). Brunner does not believe that there is a common essence of religion of which Christianity is the best example. He is very determined in his insistence on the uniqueness and absolute character of Christianity summed up in the expression, "the Word became flesh." He examines such non-Christian religions as Islam, Judaism, and Buddhism, concluding that all fall short of the unique irrepeatable revelation of the Christian faith. "No 'other religion' can assert revelation in the radical, unconditional sense in which the Christian faith does this, because no 'other religion' knows the God who is Himself the Revealer" (*ibid.*, p. 236).

Next he turns to the attempts to explain Christianity and religion psychologically and sociologically and affirms that all such attempts fail to do justice to the Christian religion. He comments: "Everyone who has some knowledge of the Christian faith is aware, without further argument, that no purely naturalistic theory which derives it from fear, or desire, or need is adequate" (*ibid.*, p. 245). All such attempts of explanation explain something, but not Christianity (*ibid.*, p. 256).

In discussing "Revelation and Religion" he comes close to Calvin by asserting that an original revelation is behind all religion exerting a pressure, but due to man's sinfulness the religious product is notoriously non-Christian. To Brunner, original revelation does not mean a revelation given to Adam. It means the presuppositions of individual and collective existence which face every generation (*ibid.*, p. 262). Original sin is man's reaction to original revelation defined in this sense. It is not some event of long ago but everyman's reaction to original revelation which is at the same time an act of apostasy.

In speaking to the question whether there is truth in other religions, Brunner pens the following strong paragraph: "Jesus Christ is both the Fulfillment of all religion and the Judgment on all religion. As the Fulfiller, He is the Truth which these religions seek in vain. There is no phenomenon in the history of religion that does not point toward Him: the bloody sacrifice of expiation, the sacred meal, the ecstatic element, the seeking of the Holy Spirit, the magical element, the indication of the *dynamis* of God in the reality of His revelation, prayer, the divine Father and the divine Judge. All this the world of religions knows in a fragmentary and distorted form, as almost unrecognizable 'relics' of an 'original' revelation. From the standpoint of Jesus Christ, the non-Christian religions seem like stammering words from some half-forgotten saying. None of them is without a breath of the Holy, and yet none of them is the Holy. None is without its impressive truth, and yet none of them is the Truth; for their Truth is Jesus Christ" (*ibid.*, p. 270).

Barth writes about "The Abolition of Religion" (*CD*, I/2, § 17). Barth examines the possibility of an essence of religion or a natural religion and rejects them both in favor of the complete uniqueness and autonomy of the Christian revelation. He writes that "we must not try to know and define and assess man and his religion as it were in advance and independently. We must not ascribe to him any existence except in possession of Christ. We must not treat of him in any other sphere than that of His kingdom, in any other relationship than that of "subordination to Him'" (*ibid.*, p. 296).

Following this, Barth announces the amazing thesis that religion is unbelief (*ibid.*, p. 299). If this is not strong enough he adds that "the piety of man is vain blasphemy and the greatest of all the sins that he commits" (*ibid.*, p. 300). Divine revelation stands in judgment over all religion. The reason is that "in religion man bolts and bars himself against revelation by providing a substitute, by taking away in advance the very thing which has been given by God" (*ibid.*, p. 303).

Tillich's discussion of religions is very critical of Brunner, who starts out with final revelation in Christ and thus looks down on all sub-standard religions (*ST*, p. 221n). Tillich's position is that wherever there is ultimate concern God in principle is recognized. Therefore all religions are to be evaluated by final revelation — not condemned — and this includes even the Christian theologian.

The classic treatment is H. Kraemer's *The Christian Message in a Non-Christian World* in which he discusses how a missionary convinced of the uniqueness of revelation in Christ witnesses in a non-Christian community with its non-Christian religion.

RESURRECTION OF CHRIST

Barth presents his doctrine of the atonement as the Judge judged in our place. He follows this with a discussion of the doctrine of the resurrection entitled "The Verdict of the Father" (CD, IV/1, 283-357). Barth sets out five criteria to which a second, complementing act of the atonement must conform and then shows how the resurrection so conforms (ibid., pp. 297ff.). His summary statement is that "the resurrection is marked off from the death of Jesus Christ as a new and specific act of God by the fact that in it there is pronounced the verdict of God the Father on the obedience of the Son: His gracious and almighty approval of the Son's representing of the human race; His acceptance of His suffering and death as it took place for the race; the justification of the will of the Father who sent the Son into the world for this purpose, of the Son who willed to submit to this will, and of the totality of sinful men as brought to an end in the death of this their Representative" (ibid., p. 354). That Christ was risen from the dead in a literal sense is expressed by Barth in the following words: "If Jesus Christ is not risen — bodily, visibly, audibly, perceptibly, in the same concrete sense in which He died, as the texts themselves have it — if He is not also risen, then our preaching and our faith are vain and futile; we are still in our sins" (ibid., pp. 351f.).

Brunner accepts Paul's witness in I Cor. 15 as the oldest and most reliable account of the resurrection (D, II, 365ff.). He is not so much interested in the empty tomb as in the appearance of the risen Lord. It was these appearances that really brought home to the disciples the reality of the risen Christ. The discrepancies of the Gospel accounts are something we ought to acknowledge in historical honesty, but the fact of the resurrection no one may doubt. Brunner does not believe in the resurrection of the flesh but of the body. The resurrection of the body does not mean that the physical body is transmuted into a spiritual body but "it means the continuity of the individual personality on this side, and on that, of death" (ibid., p. 372).

Next he opens up the question whether we believe in the resurrection because we believe the records or believe the records because we have met the living Lord. He clearly accepts the latter as the case. He accepts no ·fundamentalist historicizing or literalizing of the accounts. He says any Christian knows that he believes in the resurrection because he knows Christ as the living Lord. Thus faith in the risen Christ is really a conjunction of the total witness of the apostles and the believing encounter of the Christian with Christ.

Niebuhr's account of the resurrection is puzzling. He agrees with Baillie that mere immortality of the soul does not do justice to the richness of the biblical notion of the resurrection of the dead. On the other hand, he steers away from "literalistic corruptions" (*NDM*, II, 297) of the doctrine and prefers to speak of the resurrection of the body as a biblical symbol. The basic idea seems to be that the importance of the doctrine is not in any miraculous raising of the body but that the triumph of God is trans-historical and that it involves the fulness of man's historical existence. Whereas the old orthodox view concentrated on the body, and the liberal view on that part of man which was worthy of immortality, Niebuhr concentrates on the richness of the personality in its survival.

Tillich lists four theories about the resurrection (*ST*, II, 153ff.). In a preliminary way it must be said that the resurrection is both event and symbol and any interpretation that does not include both is unsatisfactory. First is the theory that Jesus rose physically from the dead. The difficulty with this theory is that it is a rationalization of the event. It identifies the resurrection with the absence or presence of a body. "Then the absurd question arises as to what happened to the molecules which comprise the corpse of Jesus of Nazareth. Then absurdity becomes compounded into blasphemy" (*ibid.*, pp. 155f.). Second is the spiritualistic interpretation. Jesus' soul appears to men and proves that he is still alive. But this is mere immortality of the soul. The resurrection appearances included the total personality of Christ "which includes the bodily expression of his being" (*ibid.*, p. 156). Third is that the resurrection was a psychological experience. The resurrection is that which happened in the mind of the followers of Jesus. But this does not satisfy the event-character of the resurrection.

Tillich advocates the fourth theory, the restitution theory — which is difficult to separate sharply from the psychological theory — in which "in an ecstatic experience the concrete picture of Jesus of Nazareth became indissolubly united with the reality of the New Being" (*ibid.*, p. 157). The disciples had found New Being in Christ. His death seemed to end this New Being, which is in itself contradictory. But then after his death in an ecstatic experience they identify the New Being permanently with their previous picture of Jesus of Nazareth as Jesus as the Christ. Thus Jesus is permanently associated with the concept of New Being and this is the resurrection.

Bultmann does not believe in the resurrection of corpses (*KM*, p. 8). The resurrection is not a historical event of the same order as the cross. Rather it is the obverse side of the cross. The cross represents dying with Christ to the old, inauthentic life and the resurrection means rising with Christ to the new authentic life. Historical science does not prove the resurrection but establishes the report that the disciples so believed in the resurrection. In reality the resurrection is the word of preaching, namely, the promise of new life in Christ through God's love and grace and by faith in the kerygma (*ibid.*, pp. 38-43).

An attempt to reopen the question of the resurrection on the basis of "historical reason" paralleling Kant's structuring of reason is offered in R. R. Niebuhr's *RHR*.

REVELATION

Prior to the advent of the neo-orthodox and existentialist movement we may plot three schools of revelation: (1) The high orthodox view of revelation, which considered that Scripture was virtually a pure book of revelation. In this view the Scriptures are all gold and can be melted and recast into the form of a systematic theology. There is no difference between the words of Scripture and revelation except for the qualifying remark that unregenerate men do speak within the inspired pages. (2) A modified orthodox view, which placed revelation and redemption close together. Scripture cannot be looked upon as a pure deposit of revelation but as the cognitive element of the more comprehensive program of salvation. Such views were expressed by such divergent men as J. C. K. von Hofmann, *IB*, and A. Kuyper, *PST*. It is also recently defended by Bernard Ramm in *RWG*. (3) A liberal view, which tended to consider revelation as experience or insight. If a religious experience is looked at subjectively it is insight; if looked at objectively it is revelation. Thus revelation was moral and spiritual insight into the nature of God, man, and society.

Speaking in a most general way, the newer attitude towards revelation clusters around the following six theses:

(1) In basic agreement with the older theologians and in disagreement with religious liberalism, revelation is seen as an event in which God takes the initiative. Revelation cannot be equated with the best insights of man (morally or religiously) but must be seen as that which comes to man from the other side. Thus revelation issues out of God's freedom.

(2) In basic disagreement with the older theologians, the newer views do not equate the Bible nor its doctrines with revelation. The Word of God is not the Scripture itself, nor are the statements of the Scripture themselves the revelation. The newer view holds that to equate the Bible with the Word of God, and the statements within the Bible with revelation, is an objectifying and materializing of revelation. The Bible and its statements are witnesses, signs, pointers of revelation.

(3) In agreement with some of the previous theologians the newer view makes a strong connection between revelation and salvation. Revelation is the word that saves, and salvation brings us into the light of revelation. The history of revelation and the history of salvation are the same history seen from two different perspectives. This is also a profound emphasis upon special revelation. Although Barth and Brunner, for example, may differ in their understanding of general revelation they are agreed on the centrality of special revelation.

(4) More emphasis is placed upon revelatory events than upon the revealedness of Holy Scripture. Thus the revelatory event is more fundamental than the Bible. In fact the substance of revelation (and of the Bible) is made up of such events as the call of Abraham, the exodus, the deliverance from the Babylonian captivity, the death and resurrection of Christ, and the descent of the Spirit at Pentecost.

(5) Revelation is seen as a relational event. It is an event which calls for both the Speaker and the hearer. Revelation is not understood as the delivery of truths about God but as an event or an occasion or a dialogue in which God encounters man. Revelation cannot be said to have taken place unless both partners of the encounter enter into the encounter.

(6) The Word of God is God Himself. More particularly, the Word of God is Jesus Christ. Revelation is not a doctrine but it creates doctrine. It is not the Bible but it generates the

Bible. It is not history but it forms a history. Thus the center of revelation is God Himself in his speaking and acting and thus he is the content or the subject of revelation.

Bibliographies on the subject are supplied in Baillie, *IR*, and Ramm, *RWG*. Seven important contributions to the topic are found in Baillie and Martin, *R*. Barth devotes I/1 and I/2 of *CD* to revelation; Brunner discusses it in *RR* and *D*, I. Bultmann's essay "The Concept of Revelation in the NT" appears in *EF;* and Tillich discusses "Reason and Revelation" in *ST*, I, part 1.

REVELATION, BROKENNESS OF

The brokenness of revelation means that revelation can never be received in a pure form. The human factor in the human recipient is always present and diffracts the revelation. Barth speaks of the light of revelation striking man as light strikes a prism. No matter how deeply or profoundly or existentially man receives the Word of God he receives it in human act. The reception of revelation is fallible, and whatever witness to revelation man gives stands "itself in need of criticism and revision, of repeated and ever closer re-testing" (*CD*, I/1, 14). Because revelation as a human possession is in a state of brokenness, we can never assert that our human propositions correspond one for one with the nature of the Word of God (*ibid.*, p. 50). Revelation has a worldly form and because it has a worldly form it it not transparent in itself so as to be "capable of being the translucent garment or mirror of the Word of God" (*ibid.*, p. 190).

One of the logical consequences of the brokenness of Scripture as the witness to revelation is that the Scriptures contain errors. This does not hinder Barth. He writes strongly that "if God is not ashamed of the fallibility of all the human words of the Bible, of their historical and scientific inaccuracies, their theological contradictions, the uncertainty of their tradition, and, above all, their Judaism, but adopted and made use of these expressions in all their fallibility, we do not need to be ashamed when He wills to renew it to us in all its fallibility as witness, and it is mere self-will and disobedience to try to find some infallible elements in the Bible" (*ibid.*, I/2, 531).

Brunner also speaks of the brokenness of the revelation in the Bible. He writes that "here already it is evident that the

109

Revelation, General

divine Truth is a light which cannot be received by the human mind without being refracted" (*D*, I, 13). "It is a 'word' inspired by the Spirit of God; yet at the same time it is a human message; its 'human character' means that it is coloured by the frailty and imperfection of all that is human" (*ibid.*, I, 34).

Edwin Lewis propounds similar theses, especially when he speaks of freeing the Word from the words of the Bible, and of the Christian's not being bound to all the vagaries of Scripture (*BFCF*).

REVELATION, GENERAL (*see also* Natural Theology)

General revelation is that knowledge of God that man may derive from creation, man, and providence. Older writers made no distinction between natural theology and general revelation. The recent distinction is that general revelation provides the materials and natural theology is the product. Thus man in his primeval state would have had a valid general revelation that he would have interpreted in the form of a natural theology.

In modern times Pascal and Kierkegaard have spoken disparagingly of natural theology and have emphasized that the only valid knowledge of God is that which is in the face of Jesus Christ. Barth has followed through in this tradition with a vengeance. He has repeatedly attacked natural theology, particularly as defended by Roman Catholicism or religious liberalism. He refuses to grant the distinction between general revelation and natural theology.

Brunner, on the other hand, has taken a strong stand for general revelation, which he calls "original revelation" (*RR*, chap. 6). Brunner maintains that sin can be understood only as apostasy. But apostasy is a turning away from something, and that something is the original revelation of God (*ibid.*, p. 52). He states his thesis as follows: "We therefore teach a general revelation or a revelation in the Creation, because the Holy Scriptures teach it unmistakably, and we intend to teach in accordance with Scripture" (*ibid.*, p. 59). Brunner does not believe that from this general revelation a natural theology may be deduced. He and Barth are in sharpest disagreement as to which one faithfully represents Calvin.

For a discussion of general revelation in the historic Reformed tradition with interaction with the contemporary debate, see G. C. Berkouwer, *General Revelation*.

REVELATION, IMAGES OF

Austin Farrer believes that the present discussion over the inspiration of the Bible has become stalemated and needs a new approach. Recent studies in biblical criticism and theology have made obsolete the theory that the Bible is a body of revealed propositions. A second view is that revelation is in divine act and that the Scriptures are a reliable record of the divine act. But this, says Farrer, is a flat, stenographic view of the Scriptures, which fails to account for their vitality.

A third view, according to Farrer, is found in the concept of revelation by means of images. What we have in Scripture is "divine truth . . . supernaturally communicated to men in an act of inspired thinking which falls into the shape of certain images" (GV, p. 57). The Holy Spirit unites the Scriptural writer with the Head of the Church, and out of this dynamic union flow the revealed and inspired images. Farrer gives as examples of these images the Kingdom of God, the Son of Man, the return of the Son of Man, the cross and resurrection, and the Trinity.

It is true that Christ's life was a life of events. A dynamic relationship exists between the images and the events. Events without images are dumb and non-revelational; images without events are shadows; revelation is the happy conjunction of event and image. Yet another problem arises. What is the character of biblical history? Is it ordinary history occasionally illumined by flashes of images? No, it is history written by men filled with the inspiration of images. Their history might be called image-directed and image-inspired.

E. L. Mascall concurs with Farrer's theory of images (WI).

REVELATION, INDIRECT

The concepts of incognito and indirect communication and indirect revelation are bound together. It is Brunner's and Barth's conviction that a direct, unequivocal revelation would destroy the line between the divine and the human, time and eternity, God and man, and would make faith a compelled act and not a free decision. The roots of this idea are in Pascal's *Pensées*, where he argued that God made revelation clear enough so that faith could see it, yet obscure enough so that the unregenerate could not see it. Revelation is like a skiagraph — if one knows what to look for, he sees it, but if he doesn't, he sees only meaningless configurations.

Revelation has its human and earthly side, which in itself does not arouse a man's suspicions that it is a part of the event of revelation. The Scriptures are indirect revelation. It is a human book when weighed by the canons of literature. But at the same time it is something more. Revelation engenders the Scriptures, and they are a witness, a pointer, a suggestion of revelation; but they are not the revelation itself. Brunner writes that "the written word is not the primary revelation, but the secondary form of revelation" (*RR*, p. 132). And again, "the identity between the Scriptural word and God's word is indirect rather than direct" (*PR*, p. 32).

The entire weight of the concept of revelation that Barth develops is that the Christian Scriptures are a witness to revelation and not the revelation itself (*CD*, I/2). Scores of passages could be cited, but thus the following sentence will suffice: "Again it is quite impossible that there should be a direct identity between the human word of Holy Scripture and the Word of God, and therefore between the creaturely reality in itself and as such and the reality of God the Creator" (*CD*, I/2, 499).

Niebuhr, Tillich, and Bultmann reject the older supernaturalism and see revelation as an element within, or an aspect of, the course of events. In this sense their doctrine of revelation, too, may be said to be indirect.

REVELATION, PROPOSITIONAL

It was the belief of the old orthodox theologians as well as contemporary fundamentalists and evangelicals that Scripture is the Word of God written. As written, it is therefore revelation in a conceptual form. Because it is in conceptual form it may be studied and reproduced as propositions. Thus there is such a thing as (to speak in a roundabout way) propositional revelation (cf. *RWG*, pp. 159ff.).

However, the recent mood in theology is to assert that revelation is neither the Scripture as such nor the statements within the Scriptures. Thus revelation is not fundamentally conceptual or propositional. The current emphasis is upon revelation as the divine-human encounter. Barth speaks for many contemporary theologians when he writes against viewing the Bible as "a fixed total of revealed propositions to be systematised like the sections of a *corpus* of law" (*CD*, I/1, 156).   To see revelation as propositional, says Barth, is to materialize and depersonalize revelation (*ibid.*, p. 310).   However, neither Barth nor Brunner has made explicit and clear how a non-conceptual or non-propositional revelation can give rise to Christian theology.

REVELATION, SIGNS OF

Neo-orthodox theologians do not believe the Scriptures as such are directly revelation. Objectively, revelation is an event, an occasion in which man is confronted by God in redemption and salvation. Subjectively, it is the inner encounter of God with man in terms of Jesus Christ as Saviour, Lord, and Reconciler. In order to know that revelation exists — or better, is possible — there are signs which point towards it. Although we do not have revelation in tangible form we do have signs which point in its direction. Brunner does not call them signs, but forms of revelation, and lists the Old Testament, Jesus Christ, the Apostles, the New Testament, and preaching in the Church as examples (*D*, I, 19).

Barth has an extensive discussion of the signs of revelation (*CD*, I/2, 223ff.). The signs are instruments whereby God signifies and, if He wills, occasions revelation. They are not objective instruments like a hammer or shears, but signs always at the disposal of the freedom of God. The chief sign of revelation is, of course, sacred Scripture.

Bernard Ramm speaks rather of modes of revelation (*RWG*, chaps. 2-5). These are the means whereby the revelation of God actually makes contact with human consciousness.

Although Bultmann does not discuss signs as such, the whole implication of his theology is that preaching (kerygmatic preaching) is the one sign of revelation. He does say that the preaching of the Church is founded on the Scripture (*EF*, p. 168), and this would seem to imply that the Scriptures are also a sign.

Tillich, on the other hand speaks of sign-events (*ST*, I, 115) and revelatory constellations (*ibid.*, p. 118). He also speaks of "Mediums of Revelation" (*ibid.*, p. 118). Under the latter he speaks of history, groups, and individuals as media of revelation. He makes it pointedly clear that these are occurrences *within* the orderly processes of nature. In other words, he specifically excludes any kind of supernatural event as being a sign or a medium of revelation.

RISK (*see also* Leap)

Kierkegaard introduced the term risk into theology. According to Kierkegaard, the intellect may be followed up to a point, but it eventually comes to juncture where it no longer can serve. If we are to proceed in the existential territory, it must be by faith, passion, and paradox. The paradox cannot be relieved but remains in force. The self accepts the paradox in the passion of faith, but the intellect views the acceptance of the paradox as a risk. "Without risk there is no faith. Faith is precisely the contradiction between the infinite passion of the individual's inwardness and the objective uncertainty" (*CUP*, p. 182). "For without risk there is no faith, and the greater the risk the greater the faith" (*ibid.*, p. 188).

Neo-orthodox theologians generally agree with Kierkegaard that the intellect brings us to faith. Most of them make some room in their theology for the concepts of risk and of the paradoxical. Since the Word of God comes to man as a given, its acceptance by man will appear as a risk to the intellect. Bultmann also follows through with the notion of risk. The contents of faith are not provable, and therefore the act of faith will always appear as risk to the intellect (*JCM*, p. 73). The concept of risk and that of leap are virtually the same.

SAGA

Barth calls the opening chapters of the book of Genesis sagas (*CD*, III/1, 82ff.). This is how most historians would classify these materials. Barth dissociates himself from liberalism by maintaining that, although mythical materials might have entered into the materials, the accounts are not myths. He also dissociates himself from much of orthodoxy by stating that they are not ordinary history. He presents what he considers to be the theological interpretation of the chapters: that theological statements do not compete with scientific statements; for, according to Barth, the "Bible and science" issue does not exist (*ibid.*, pp. ix-x).

The literary means of writing the saga is called by Barth the divinatory and poetic. In other words it is an imaginative and poetical reconstruction of creation guided by the Holy Spirit and believed in virtue of the power of the Holy Spirit.

SCANDAL

Kierkegaard attempted vigorously to reintroduce into Christianity its original scandal. Two things in the Danish Christendom of his day were eliminating the scandal from Christianity. First, the Hegelians were rationalizing Christianity to such an extent that there was nothing left in Christianity to shock the intellect. Christianity had achieved philosophical respectability. Second, Christianity had become a way of life for all Danes. There was no social scandal in being a Christian, because everybody in Denmark was. Kierkegaard countered by showing that according to the New Testament the gospel was scandal and shock.

Brunner admits that the gospel is scandal and a folly to the non-Christian but he adds that when the gospel is accepted by faith it ceases to be scandal and folly (*RR*, p. 171). The message of the cross is not to be made reasonable for modern man but it is to encounter him as a scandal (*ibid.*, p. 166). The gospel itself is not folly and scandal, but it is such to us because "we are enmeshed in the net woven by our sinful struggles for independence" (*ibid.*, p. 175).

Niebuhr thinks Christianity is a scandal and a folly to the man who wishes to follow the pathway of strict rationality alone. These ways of rationality are always from partial perspectives (*NDM*, II, 62). Thus the cross, the resurrection, and the last judgment appear foolish to the man who does not know the wisdom of God in these things.

It could be said that Barth, too, follows the notion of scandal. Revelation confronts man in such a radical way that it cannot be anticipated by him in any way, nor controlled by man. It must come to him as a scandal.

Bultmann is also much concerned about the scandal of Christianity. Because the true gospel is clothed in Jewish and Greek myths, it unnecessarily scandalizes modern man. Modern man is scandalized by angels, demons, miracles, a three-storied universe, and the resurrection of dead bodies. These scandals must be eliminated. But the real scandal of the gospel or kerygma must be kept. The gospel as a call to new existence, to a new self-understanding, to authentic existence strikes the man who is living in the fallenness of the world as a scandal. This scandal is part of the kerygma itself and must not be removed.

SEPARATISM (*see also* Fundamentalism, -ist)

The development of religious modernism in the nineteenth century led to the penetration of most denominations by theologians, ministers, and denominational workers who held to the tenets of religious modernism. As a result, denominational programs soon reflected the influence of religious liberalism — in theology, in ethics, in preaching, and in literature. A large part of the personnel of the denominations included religious liberals, most seriously of all on the mission field.

The prevailing opinion among pastors was that something like this was inevitable. The Church was no more to be free from heretical movements than Israel was to be free from false prophets or cultic corruption of her religion (as seen so remarkably in the careers of Elijah and Elisha). Religious liberalism was to be countered by conservative men who remained in their pulpits and denominational posts and bore an evangelical witness. Withdrawal simply meant deeding over positions, power, and money to religious liberalism.

An alternative method for countering religious modernism was the approach of the separatists, who held that it is contrary to the New Testament for conservatives and liberals to work together in the same denomination. By cooperating with denominational structures the conservative adds to the theological confusion of the times. By giving to the denominational program the conservative gives his money to finance religious liberals. Therefore, the separatist believes, the only remedy is for the conservatives to separate from the apostate denomination and form pure churches and pure denominational structures. By such means the concepts of a pure church and a pure denomination are realistically approximated.

SHATTERING

Kierkegaard protested that neither the philosophy of religion nor the Danish religion of his day called for a radical transformation of the individual. But true Christianity calls for this radical transformation, which is based upon a shattering of the self. Kierkegaard speaks of infinite resignation, using the word "infinite" in the sense of the extreme, the ultimate, the final (*FT*). Thus infinite resignation is supreme resignation. It is the resignation from the wrong notion and the wrong method of seeking eternal happiness. In it there is more than repentance, for repentance means turning away from specific sins. Infinite resignation meant for Kierkegaard the total movement of the self away from a way of life that was supposed to lead to happiness. It involves the shattering of the individual's false method of existence, and a preparation for the way of faith.

Niebuhr follows Kierkegaard in this notion of shattering. With Kierkegaard he agrees that metaphysical and rational truth does not shatter (*NDM*, II, 61). To be shattered means to be robbed of all one's false securities, one's pride, and one's power. It means having one's anxiety heightened to the point of despair.

Brunner also has something to say about shattering. He writes that "only he who allows himself thus to be shattered, and thus be crucified with Christ, is able to receive what God wills to give him at the cross" (*RR*, p. 116; cf. D, I, 125).

SIGNS OF REVELATION, see Revelation, Signs of

SIN

Kierkegaard says that sin posits itself. This means that there is no cause for sin save sin itself. He repeatedly calls it the qualitative leap, which "no science has explained nor can explain" (*COD*, p. 55). "By the qualitative leap sin came into the world, and in this way is continually coming into it" (*ibid.*, p. 99). Sin is the result of man's using his freedom to find security in some human, finite thing rather than relying totally upon God. His freedom makes him dizzy in view of the possibilities it unveils, and in this dizziness man makes the fatal leap to a creaturely security. Thus sin posits itself, and is not the product of some more primeval cause.

Brunner has written much on the doctrine of sin. He discusses man in the contradiction of sin (*MIR*, chaps. 6 and 7). He repeatedly refers to human sinfulness (*D*, II, chap. 3; cf. *RR*, pp. 50f.). Brunner begins with the methodological principle that we are not to start with Genesis 3 but with the New Testament. Furthermore, our sinfulness, personal and corporate, is known only in Christ. He announces his Christological principle as follows: "Only *in Christ*, that is, as believers, do we see the solidarity of sin to which we belong; only in Christ do we know that we are united in His redemption" (*D*, II, 99).

117

Brunner spells out the characteristics of sin. It is rebellion. Sin is not the first thing about man but the second. "Sin is not the primary phenomenon, it is not the beginning, but it is a turning-away from the beginning, the abandonment of the origin, the break with that which God has given and established" (*ibid.*, p. 91). Sin is apostasy. "Sin is emancipation from God, giving up the attitude of dependence, in order to try to win full independence, which makes man equal with God" (*ibid.*, p. 93). Sin is a total act. It is an act which determines the total existence of man. "It means that man declares his whole existence to be 'free,' the whole man shakes off all the bonds which tie him to God" (*ibid.*, p. 93). Sin is universal. Because Brunner rejects the Fall in the sense of a historical event in which one man brought all men into sin, he has more trouble being specific about the universality of sin than about the other characteristics of sin. In the final analysis it is a mystery (*ibid.*, p. 97). His point seems to be that we reckon backwards. Just as we recognize the solidarity of the redeemed in Christ, so we must presuppose the solidarity of the lost in sin. In agreement with Kierkegaard he says that each man is individual man and humanity.

Niebuhr's doctrine of sin is not materially different from Brunner's. He writes: "Sin is thus the unwillingness of man to acknowledge his creatureliness and dependence upon God and his effort to make his own life independent and secure" (*NDM*, I, 137). He locates sin in the pride of man, which is not some simple bit of vanity but man's total over-estimation of himself. He also indicates that the depravity of man and the universality of sin are verifiable from experience. If reason could master sin, we would be done with sin; but the evidence to date counts to the opposite, so modern man must still reckon with sin as depravity and with the universality of sin even though education and social engineering may bring amelioration (*HCT*, pp. 348-351).

Barth's contribution to the doctrine of sin is methodological. He locates his doctrine of sin not between the doctrine of man and the doctrine of salvation as in traditional theology but in the midst of his doctrine of reconciliation (*CD*, IV/1, § 60, "The Pride and Fall of Man").

Barth denies two theses of a methodological nature. (1) We cannot go from a human sense of imperfection, inadequacy, etc., to a doctrine of sin. The ordinary man's sense of his imperfection is not the same as the sense of sin (*ibid.*, p. 360). (2) We cannot discuss a doctrine of sin and then proceed to a doctrine of atonement in Christ as the cure for sin. We cannot have a doctrine of sin prior to a Christology. Barth believes only in a Christological doctrine of sin. His basic thesis is contained in the following sentence: "It is a matter of the knowledge of the one God who in His Word became flesh for us, and therefore of the knowledge of His truth in this one revelation, and therefore of the one indivisible knowledge of the Christian faith, the basis and subject which is God in his atoning work, and therefore God in Jesus Christ. The knowledge of human sin is enclosed in this knowledge" (*ibid.*, p. 389). As far as sin is concerned, "sin is that which is absurd, man's absurd choice and decision for that which is not, described in the Genesis story as his hearkening to the voice of the serpent, the beast of chaos. Sin exists only in this absurd event" (*ibid.*, p. 410).

Tillich has a lengthy discussion of sin in all its aspects in *ST*, II, 29-78. The most important part of his treatment is his concept of estrangement. He says that Hegel discovered the term. In estrangement man belongs to that which he is estranged from. Thus man belongs to the ground of his being even though in sin man is not in communion with God. Thus this estrangement is the essence of sin. But estrangement cannot displace sin in Christian language. Estrangement is the general nature of sin. But sin is also wilful, personal act. And only as we retain the word sin do we retain this personal, wilful character of the sinful act.

SOBORNOST

Sobornost is a term used in the Russian Orthodox Church and is considered untranslatable. "Fellowship" and "group-consciousness" approximate its meaning. It is the feeling of oneness and communion which all worshippers have towards the assembled Church during the performance of the liturgy. This quality of sobornost distinguishes the Russian Church from the authoritarianism of Roman Catholicism and the individualism of Protestantism (*ODCC*, p. 1266).

SPECTATOR

A spectator is a person who views a contest but does not enter into it, whereas a participant is a person engaged in the contest. Kierkegaard pilloried the spectator attitude towards Christianity

119

and demanded the existential commitment (*AC*). Much of contemporary theology follows Kierkegaard in affirming that the reality of Christianity is never known by the spectator but only by the participant. Thus Karl Heim writes that "a proposition or a truth is said to be existential when I cannot apprehend it or assent to it from the standpoint of a mere spectator, but only on the ground of my total existence" (quoted in *CA*, p. 51n). Bultmann says that man cannot see the meaning of history as a spectator but only in his responsible decisions (*HE*, p. 155). Barth makes a strong distinction between being a spectator and being obedient. Only the man in obedience has the true knowledge of God (*CD*, II/1, 26).

SPIRIT

Spirit is one of the terms of Kierkegaard's existentialist terminology. "Christianity is spirit, spirit is inwardness, inwardness is subjectivity, subjectivity is essentially passion, and in its maximum an infinite, personal, passionate interest in one's eternal happiness" (*CUP*, p. 33). More specifically, spirit in man is the synthesis of the temporal and the eternal, of the body and soul (*COD*, p. 76). Animals do not have spirit and are not capable of existential experience. Carnell, commenting on Kierkegaard, defines spirit as follows: "Spirit is the power of self-transcendence. . . . Man *is* the truth, i.e., he has risen to the existential assignment, only when he reflects the eternal in time. Spirit is freedom, and freedom is choice. The eternal *becomes* time, therefore, only in the *instant* that passionate inward decision materializes" (*PCR*, p. 458).

Niebuhr also speaks of man as spirit. Spirit is man's self-transcendence and world-transcendence (*NDM*, I, 14). Later he writes: "Man as spirit transcends the temporal and natural process in which he is involved and also transcends himself" (*ibid.*, p. 251).

Barth has a long discussion of man as spirit (*CD*, III/2, 344ff.). "Man exists because he has spirit" (*ibid.*, p. 344). "Man has spirit. By putting it in this way we describe the spirit as something that comes to man, something not essentially his own but to be received by him, something that totally limits his constitution and thus totally determines him" (*ibid.*, p. 354). "Spirit is, in the most general sense, the operation of God upon His creation, and especially the movement of God towards man. Spirit is thus the principle of man's relation to God, of man's fellowship with him" (*ibid.*, p. 356).

SPIRIT, WITNESS OF

Although it has been claimed that Calvin and Luther replaced the pope with the Scriptures, the truth of the matter is that the teaching magisterium of the Roman Catholic Church is replaced by the Holy Spirit. In *Bondage of the Will* Luther spoke of the inner clarity of the Scriptures, by which he meant their illumination of the Holy Spirit. In Book One of the *Institutes* Calvin systematized the doctrine of the witness of the Spirit.

This witness focuses first on the sense of divine sonship of the believer and then on the Scriptures as the source of the gospel of the good news of divine sonship. Although post-Reformation dogmaticians on both the Reformed and Lutheran side carried over the doctrine it lost its vitality. The supernatural character of the Scriptures themselves was so emphasized that the witness of the Spirit seemed to have no proper function. Liberalism had no means of doing justice to this doctrine, for it denied the supernatural revelation and redemption upon which it rests. Fundamentalism was only a step removed from liberalism, for in so emphasizing the verbal inspiration of Scripture and the inerrancy of Scripture it also embarrassed the role of the witness of the Spirit.

However, the doctrine came to life again in the work of such Reformed theologians as Kuyper (*PST*), Lecerf (*IRD*), and Warfield, who wrote much on Calvin's knowledge of God. Bernard Ramm (*WS*) has attempted to carry on this tradition and interpret it in the light of recent theology.

In their attempts to rediscover the insights of the Reformers, the neo-orthodox theologians, too, have returned to the doctrine of the witness of the Spirit. In *RR* Brunner devotes an entire chapter to it (chap. 22). He opposes authoritarian Roman Catholicism, dogmatic fundamentalism, and ineffable mysticism with the doctrine of the witness of the Spirit. It is not human powers of sympathy or comprehension that enable a man to grasp the message of Christ and His cross but only the power of the Holy Spirit. It is the Spirit who leads men to Christ, and then leads them to the Bible. We do not believe in the Bible and then in Christ, but we believe in Christ and then in the Bible. "The ground, the authority, which moves me to faith

121

is no other than Jesus Christ Himself, as He speaks to me from the pages of the Scriptures through the Holy Spirit, as my Lord and my Redeemer. This is what men of old used to call the *testimonium spiritus sancti internum*" (*ibid.*, p. 170). But the witness of the Spirit is not an *imprimatur* on everything in the Bible. It is limited to that which pertains to the Father and the Son. Thus the Christian is not bound to the world of the facts of the Bible (*ibid.*, p. 175).

Barth also has a doctrine of the witness of the Spirit although he does not always label his doctrine that way. He does refer now and again to the witness of the Spirit. But more important are his massive treatments of the Holy Spirit in *CD*. The first is in I/1, where he discusses the Holy Spirit as the revealedness of revelation. The second is in IV/1, 643, where he deals with the doctrine of reconciliation. He returns again to the subject in IV/2, 125ff. making it clear that the risen and ascended Lord is recognized as such only in virtue of the witness of the Spirit.

STATE

Oscar Cullmann argues for a Christological foundation of the state. The lordship of Christ is universal. In addition to the specific, soteriological lordship of Christ in the Church, there is also His wider lordship in the world. Unless we grant this we cannot be in harmony with the statements in the New Testament assigning universal lordship to Christ. Pressing harder, Cullmann argues that Christ is lord of the powers who are the angelic lords of political bodies. This is what he means by the Christological foundation of the state (*CT*, p. 202). C. F. H. Henry reviews Cullmann's position and rejects it ("State," *BDT*, p. 501).

SUBJECTIVITY

Subjectivity is a notion introduced by Kierkegaard and can be found in some form in all theologians influenced by existentialism. Subjectivity is "an inner transformation, an actualization of inwardness . . . infinite passionate interest" (*CUP*, p. 51). To be subjective in the Kierkegaardian sense is to "become a subject in truth" for "passion is subjectivity" (*ibid.*, p. 117). "Subjectivity is truth, subjectivity is reality" (*ibid.*, p. 306). Inwardness, passion, infinite interest, are all synonyms of subjectivity. Carnell states: "While it may seem confusing to hear Kierkegaard speak of truth as 'subjectivity,' what he actually means is the subjectivist state of ethical decision, not that odious subjectivity which characterizes skepticism. Subjectivity is infinite passionate concern; it is the being of becoming, the attaining of the existential assignment" (*PCR*, p. 463). As Carnell indicates there is a difference between subjectivity and subjectivism. Subjectivism involves the relativity of knowledge; subjectivity is the character of an existential communication.

SUBSTANCE CRITICISM

The term "substance criticism" (German, *Sachkritik*) is not current in English or American theology, but it has been a subject of debate among the continental theologians. Substance criticism means that an interpreter, after determining the meaning (*i.e.*, the substance) of a passage of Scripture, may yet criticize this meaning, and accept or reject it. Those who deny substance criticism affirm that after an exegete has determined the meaning of the passage using all the methods of scholarship and criticism available, he is bound by Christian conscience to accept the teaching or substance of the passage.

Historically, orthodoxy has stood against substance criticism. It believed that once the teachings of Scripture were ascertained the Christian was bound to them. Religious liberalism on the other hand believed in substance criticism. A religious liberal might well grant that the New Testament teaches the bodily resurrection of Christ or the virgin birth but he is not bound to believe it.

The issue has broken out afresh between Barth and Bultmann. Bultmann maintains the right of substance criticism and Barth denies it. The issue is complicated by the fact that it is not always easy to determine the difference between criticism as such and substance criticism. Brunner, for example, rejects the virgin birth while maintaining the incarnation. Again Tillich and Niebuhr accept certain passages of Scripture in a symbolic sense but not in a literal sense. Niebuhr does not accept a literal return of Christ, but he interprets the return of Christ as symbolizing the truth that man's supreme and final happiness lies outside of history.

SUICIDE

Tillich considers suicide as one of the important theological problems of today. It is despair which leads to suicide, and sui-

123

cide is therefore a concept wider than that of the violent taking of one's own life. There are many forms of self-negation of life which are suicidal even though they do not end in the violent act itself. Tillich lists five suicidal conditions in addition to the act of self-annihilation (*ST*, II, 75f.). But suicide is always a temporal solution, whether it be the violent act itself or whether it be a form of spiritual or psychological suicide in the form of the negation of life. Only the answer of eternity really answers the problem of despair.

Barth has written on suicide in great detail dealing with Scriptural instances (*CD*, III/4, 401ff.). His basic answer is that life belongs to God and is given to man as a loan. Therefore man does not have a right to take it. Barth sees suicide not only as despair but as the most radical attempt of man that there is to get justice and freedom (*ibid.*, p. 403). The basic answer is not that man must live but that he may live. "This is the biblical contribution to the problem of suicide. It states indirectly but so much the more clearly where and on what assumption suicide is impossible and excluded. It is excluded by the grace of God, by the cross and resurrection of Jesus, in which the sin of rebellion against the grace of God is expiated and abolished once for all, and God as Creator, Giver and Lord of life has fundamentally and conclusively said Yes to man" (*ibid.*, p. 409).

SYMBOL

Tillich is the contemporary theologian who has given most attention to a doctrine of theological symbolism. In one terse paragraph he sets forth his apologetics for symbolism (*ST*, I, 238; cf. *TPT*, pp. 333ff.). Tillich bases his doctrine of symbolism on his doctrine of God. He says that we may make one literal statement about God: God is being itself. All other statements about God are symbolic. God as being itself is thus the ground of all the structures in being. Therefore the structures in some way reflect backward to the nature of God. He calls this the analogy of being in reverse. Therefore we may take one of these structures and use it symbolically for an assertion about God.

But Tillich is worried that a sign is confused with a symbol. A sign is a purely arbitrary item, but a symbol participates in the reality which it symbolizes. A representative example is God as our Father. "If God is symbolized as 'Father,' he is brought down to the human relationship of father and child. But at the same time this human relationship is consecrated into a pattern of the divine relationship. If 'Father' is employed as a symbol for God, fatherhood is seen in its theonomous, sacramental depth" (*ST*, I, 240).

Symbols may come into existence and die out. The important thing is that symbols cannot be artificially chosen. Tillich does not specify how they are chosen, but he implies that they are chosen in a dynamic situation in which some aspect of God is grasped afresh in some element of the world.

SYMBOLIC ESCHATOLOGY, *see* Eschatology

SYSTEM

Hegel postulated Being as the fundamental category and from it attempted to deduce the table of categories for the universe. In addition, he propounded a system of ontological logic, namely that of thesis, antithesis, and synthesis. Although he did not attempt to account for every particular fact, Hegel did attempt to give an explanation of the development of the major factors of Western culture. With proper reservations one could say that Hegel attempted to systematize the universe.

This drive for system in Hegel infuriated Kierkegaard, and he poured out some of his bitterest scorn on The System, as he called it. He opposed The System on two counts. First, it is without passion. Since there is no inwardness nor subjectivity in The System, man is not really man in it. The man of The System is a fantastic being. Secondly, The System cannot explain the oddities of human existence — a sneeze, a patch on the elbow of a coat, the necessity of picking up one's paycheck.

Kierkegaard believed that for a system to be a system it had to be closed (*CUP*, p. 98). If a philosopher could not close his system, he had no system. Kierkegaard would admit that the universe was a system to God but not to an existing individual (*ibid.*, pp. 99, 107). Therefore, Kierkegaard ridiculed the grandiose claim to system by the Hegelians at every opportunity. A faint echo of his protest can be heard in both Barth and Brunner, who vigorously oppose the idea of system in theology.

TELEOLOGICAL ESCHATOLOGY, see Eschatology

THEISTIC PROOFS

Theistic proofs are philosophical arguments for the existence of God. If the argument is drawn from some aspect of man, such as his reason, his knowledge, or his moral life, it is called an *a priori* proof; if it is drawn from the universe, such as from motion, causation, or design, it is called an *a posteriori* proof. Usually from the theistic proofs a natural theology is constructed.

The great Western tradition has been that of Anselm and St. Thomas Aquinas. Anselm is famous for his *a priori* ontological argument, and St. Thomas is famous for his fivefold *a posteriori* proof. Thomism today, both within and outside the Roman Catholic Church, accepts the validity of St. Thomas's proofs.

Pascal was one of the first of the modern thinkers to reject theistic proofs on the grounds that they make use of reason in a territory where only the heart prevails. Therefore he was not interested in the God of philosophers but in the God of Abraham, Isaac, and Jacob. Kierkegaard follows hard on his heels. He says that the proofs fail to produce certainty, and religion without certainty is unthinkable (*COD*, p. 125). Again, he claims to be unsure that he could fashion a proof, and if he did he would live in torment for fear he had made a mistake in the proof (*PF*, p. 33). In another place he states that God is not present in nature (*CUP*, p. 218). God is in nature, but secretly, not openly. The open revelation of God is paganism, not Christianity.

In Barth's rejection of the analogy of being he rejects all the *a posteriori* proofs for God's existence. Barth's great treatment of the existence of God is to be found in *CD*, II/1. Man's knowledge of God is in no sense man's achievement. If man has a knowledge of God it means that God has created it within him. Barth takes his stance in the freedom of God, the grace of God, and the revelation of God. God in His freedom has the power and authority to make Himself known. Therefore if we know God, it is in virtue of the freedom of God (cf. "God Before Man," *ibid.*, pp. 31ff.; and "The Knowability of God," *ibid.*, pp. 63ff.). Secondly, "It is only by the grace of God that it comes about that God is knowable to us" (*ibid.*, p. 69). Thus Barth rejects the Roman Catholic methodology (*ibid.*, p. 79ff.). Finally, God is known in His self-revelation so that we might say that the proof for the existence of God is that God in revelation makes

Himself known. One citation is sufficient: "Knowledge of God can always proceed only from the knowledge of His existence in a two-fold sense that we always already have this knowledge and that we must have it from God Himself, in order consequently to know Him" (*ibid.*, p. 39).

Brunner's basic thesis is that the only vital knowledge of God is that which comes by revelation through Jesus Christ. A philosophical knowledge of God, if possible, is abstract, theoretical, speculative, and does not call for commitment on behalf of man (*RR*, chap. 22, "The Proof of the Existence of God").

Although the proofs do not impress brilliant philosophers, and although they come short of the biblical revelation, Brunner is not totally against them. The one position in philosophy he considers bereft of any support is materialism. But brilliant minds are always returning to the idea of God. One cannot say, then, that God is dead. Brunner reviews the traditional proofs and shows what elements in Christian faith they anticipate. His basic stance may be gained from the following: "From the standpoint of the Christian faith there are two things to be said about the proofs for the existence of God in general. First, faith has no interest in them. The way in which the divine revelation produces the certainty of faith is quite different from that of proof, and it is completely independent of the success or failure of the process of proof. Secondly, the content of the knowledge 'secured' by these proofs is something quite different from the content of the knowledge of God. The 'God' of the proofs for the existence of God is not the Living God of faith, but an intellectual abstraction, an 'Idea,' and 'Absolute,' a 'Highest,' or 'Necessary Being,' the 'Unconditioned Value,' *et cetera,* an entity whose concept may perhaps be brought into agreement with the God of faith, but which never evokes it" (*RR*, pp. 340f.).

THEOLOGICAL LANGUAGE

In the 1920's a new version of positivism emerged in the city of Vienna among philosophers of the so-called Vienna Circle. The movement, first called logical positivism, took the recently-developed mathematical logic and used it as a means of investigating sentences. The name logical positivism reflects both its use of logic and its radical empirical nature. At first it attempted the logical analysis of the sentences of science, but it became apparent that such a program called for more, and the movement was changed to logical empiricism, which made an effort to correlate terms in a sentence with sense data. Enlargement again took place, especially among British philosophers, and the broad general movement became known as analytic philosophy.

One of the general presuppositions of the analytic school is that the meaning of a sentence is the method by which it is verified. Thus sentences could be verified or falsified. But if a sentence could not be verified or falsified it was meaningless. Religious sentences, ethical sentences, poetic sentences, and value-judgment sentences offered no means of verification and were so judged as meaningless. The classical essay on this subjects is in A. J. Ayer's *Language, Truth and Logic*, chapter 6.

This constituted a real challenge to those theologians who were keenly aware of the modern developments in philosophy. The most vocal of these theologians have been from Oxford University. From these men and others there has emerged a significant body of literature which attempts to correlate theology with the new analytic philosophy.

It is of historical importance to note that Barth commenced his serious work in his dogmatics with the problem of language. His first major thesis in *CD*, I/1, is: "As a theological discipline, dogmatics is the scientific test to which the Christian Church puts herself regarding the language about God which is peculiar to her" (*ibid.*, p. 1).

In the current debate about the nature of theological language theologians have described theological language by the terms convictional language, revelational language, odd language, oblique language, parabolic language, symbolic language, story language, mythological language, and image language.

For further study of this highly technical subject the following bibliography is offered.

History and General Position

The Concise Encyclopedia of Western Philosophy and Philosophers.

H. Feigl, "Logical Empiricism," *Twentieth-Century Philosophy*, pp. 371ff.

Joergen Joergensen, "The Development of Logical Empiricism," *International Encyclopedia of Unified Science*, II/9.

J. O. Urmson, *Philosophical Analysis: Its Development Between the Two Wars.*

Attempts to Correlate Analytic Philosophy and Theology

Gordon Clark, *Religion, Reason and Revelation.*
Frederick Ferré, *Language, Logic and God.*
Flew and Mcintyre, *New Essays in Philosophical Theology.*
Michael Foster, *Mystery and Philosophy.*
Ben Kimpel, *Religious Faith, Language and Knowledge.*
A. C. Macintyre, *Difficulties in Christian Belief.*
Basil Mitchel (ed.), *Faith and Logic.*
Jules Moreau, *Language and Religious Language.*
Bernard Ramm, *Special Revelation and the Word of God.*
I. Ramsey (ed.), *Prospect for Metaphysics.*
———, *Religious Language.*
N. Smart, *Reasons for Belief.*
Toulmin *et al., Metaphysical Beliefs.*
John Wilson, *Language and Christian Belief.*

Criticism, Alternate Theories

B. Blanshard, *Reason and Analysis.*
H. J. Paton, *The Modern Predicament.*
W. M. Urban, *Language and Reality.*
Philip Wheelwright, *The Burning Fountain.*

THEOLOGICAL POSITIVISM

A theological system is termed positivistic if it renounces any claim to be built upon a metaphysical or philosophical foundation, but is built immediately upon religious or theological foundations. Thus Ritschl was a theological positivist, in that he attempted to eschew metaphysics and build theology on the historical revelation in Jesus Christ. Barth and Brunner are also positivistic in that they disavow all human metaphysical systems and rest their case upon the sheer givenness of revelation (cf. Cobb, *LOCT*). Reformation theology also was positivistic in the sense that it renounced the scholastic method of the Roman Catholic theologians and taught the self-credibility (*autopistia*) of the Christian Scriptures.

THEOLOGY, NATURAL, *see* Natural Theology

Time

TIME (*see also* Kairos, Chronos)

Among the many contemporary theologians who have given much attention to the topic of "theological" time is Oscar Cullmann. Cullmann works with the schema of Holy History and traces a time line from Creation to Redemption to End-Time. Thus he attempts to chart out the biblical notion of time (*CT*, p. 82). There is time before creation; then creation; then the time of creation to the Parousia; then the continuation of the time line after the Parousia. At the center as the dramatic climax of the time process is the Mid-Point, the appearance of Jesus Christ. The time line of Holy History is composed of special dots, *kairoi*, in which time is filled with meaning.

John Marsh distinguishes between chronological time and realistic time. Modern man is concerned with the former and the biblical writers with the latter. This is founded upon the difference between *chronos* and *kairos* although the distinction of realistic time and chronological time spreads to many other words of both the Old and New Testaments ("Time," *TWB*, pp. 258-267).

Basic to all in Marsh's opinion is that God is the Lord of time whether it be called day, season, month, or year. Even in these chronological terms the biblical use is yet filled with divine meaning. Marsh writes, for example, that "it would seem, therefore, that the time of Jesus Christ was not only a fulfilment of prophetic Messianic times . . . but also a fulfilment of Exodus time. . . . Once more we see that the biblical conception of time is not that of evolution or progress or even of chronological succession: it is at bottom one of promise (prophetic and historical) and fulfilment, in which history consists of times bringing opportunities, the basic time and the decisive opportunity being that of the coming of Jesus Christ, in whom all the promises of God, prophetic and historical, are yea, Amen" (*ibid.*, p. 263).

James Barr is very critical of the basic lexical details of both Cullmann and Marsh (*BWT*).

Tillich also has a philosophy of time much like Cullmann and Marsh, in that he makes a distinction between *chronos* and *kairos* (cf. "Kairos," *HCT*, pp. 193ff.).

It is said that the only great treatment of theological time since Augustine is that of Barth, who has two major discussions of time (*CD*, I/2, 14, "The Time of Revelation"; *CD*, III/2, 47, "Man in his Time"). Barth's basic thesis is that there is such a thing as theological time but this can only be learned from a study of revelation. It is difficult to summarize Barth in a few lines, but his basic point seems to be that there is chronological time and existential time (the latter is my expression). Thus man as a sinner leads a life in lost existential time and the purpose of Christ is to save man from lost existential time to redeemed existential time. That which stands between man's fallen time and man's redeemed time is the time of Jesus Christ in which the redemption of man has occurred. Among other things Barth writes that "it is [God present], who always was and will always be and for that very reason has a genuine before and after; in other words, the active Lord of time, who in His action creates and sustains His own time out of the wretched span of this lost time of ours, the Lord before whom time can have no legality of its own, before whom the longest time is the shortest and the shortest the longest, before whom the irreversibility of time is not for one moment in an indestructable position. This mastered, this fulfilled time is the time of revelation, the time of Jesus Christ" (*ibid.*, I/1, 52f.).

For a thorough study of the biblical expressions themselves cf. Jenni, "Time," *IDB*, 642-649.

TRINITY

The most extensive treatment of the Trinity in contemporary theology is by Karl Barth, who discusses it in more than two hundred pages of his *CD* (I/1, 339ff.). Three things of major importance stand out in Barth's treatment of the Trinity. (1) The Trinity is located in theological prolegomena rather than in the doctrine of God where it usually occurs. (2) It is discussed fundamentally from the perspective of revelation: "God's Word is God Himself in His revelation. For God reveals Himself as the Lord, and that according to Scripture signifies for the concept of revelation that God Himself in unimpaired unity yet also in unimpaired difference is Revealer [Father], Revelation [Son], and Revealedness [Holy Spirit]" (*ibid.*, p. 339). (3) The use of the word "person" is rejected because of the radical change in its meaning since the days of the first trinitarian formulation. Modalism is also rejected. Barth prefers the German word *Weise*. "This distinction or arrangement is the distinction or arrangement of three 'Persons' — we prefer to say, the three 'modes of being' in God" (*ibid.*, p. 407).

131

Brunner expresses his opinion of the doctrine of the Trinity in the form of the following thesis: "The ecclesiastical doctrine of the Trinity, established by the dogma of the ancient Church, is not a Biblical *kerygma,* therefore it is not the *kerygma* of the Church, but it is a theological doctrine which defends the central faith of the Bible and of the Church. Hence it does not belong to the sphere of the Church's message, but it belongs to the sphere of theology; in this sphere it is the work of the Church to test and examine its message, in the light of the Word of God given to the Church. Certainly in this process of theological reflection the doctrine of the Trinity is central" (*D,* I, 206). Thus the Trinity is a second-order doctrine and is a doctrine which protects the kerygma. Furthermore, Brunner is not at all happy with the formalized doctrine of the Trinity in the Athanasian Creed.

Tillich prefers to speak of trinitarian principles rather than of the doctrine of the Trinity as historically understood (*ST,* I, 250f.). The Father means that God is the abyss of the divine, the element of power. It is God in his majesty, in the unapproachable intensity of his being, the inexhaustible ground of being in which everything has its origin. The Son as the Logos is the principle of meaning, structure, and objectification. It is God speaking in his word. The Spirit is the principle of creativity. The Spirit proceeds from the divine ground to the creation, and yet in turn unites creation to its divine ground. These lines of Tillich are difficult to condense and just as difficult to understand. But there appears to be no Athanasian doctrine of one God in three Persons but rather one God in a complexity of relationships to creation.

A recent work which surveys the historical and contemporary materials on the Trinity is Claude Welch's *In This Name.*

ULTIMATE CONCERN

"Ultimate concern" is part of the vocabulary of Paul Tillich's existentialism. In discussing the formal criteria of theology he lists ultimate concern as one of these criteria (*ST,* I, 11ff.). An ultimate concern is contrasted with a preliminary concern, which may be a judgment in art, a belief in some theory in physics, a theory of medical healing, some thought about social reconstruction or international war. On the other hand, an ultimate concern is unconditioned. It is independent of any conditions of character, desire, or circumstances. Furthermore, it is a total concern. It does not allow for the exclusion of any part of ourselves or our world. Yet again, it is an infinite concern. It does not allow for relaxation or rest.

That which is of ultimate concern demands the ultimate in response, which is total surrender, our infinite passion, the total yielding of our subjective passion. From this, Tillich draws the conclusion that only those theological propositions are allowable whose object demands ultimate or total concern. Thus to love God with all our heart, our soul, our mind, and our strength is an ultimate concern because it demands from us the totality of our love.

Ultimate concern, furthermore, has to do with our being or non-being. These expressions must be existentially interpreted. Tillich defines being existentially as meaning "the whole of human reality, the structure, the meaning, and the aim of existence" (*ibid.*, I, 14). Thus being would be our authentic existential existence, and non-being our inauthentic existential existence.

UNITY OF DOCTRINE

The goal of Reformed theology was to systematize the revelation of God as one unitary corpus of revelation. It considered that there was one system of doctrine under the literary diversity and historical records. In the English speaking world it was considered that the Westminster Confession best represented that one system of theology which underlay the Sacred Scriptures. The *Book of Concord* played a similar role among the Lutherans.

It was the belief of many religious liberals that there was not one theology behind Sacred Scripture but several theologies. Even in the New Testament there was no consistent theological viewpoint. Thus the notion of a theological unity of the Scriptures was broken.

However, Barth and Brunner have attempted anew to find some sort of unity in the theology of the Scriptures. This is not done by reviving the older Reformed view, nor is the theological diversity of Scripture denied. Brunner has a radial theory of the unity of the Bible. He writes that "there is a Synoptic, a Pauline, and a Johannine type of doctrine; each differs considerably from the other, and no theological art reduces them to the same common denominator. What they all have in common is this:

Universalism

He Himself, Jesus Christ, is the Word of God; He is the center
of their testimony; but their witness to Him . . . are like radii
which point toward this center from different angles, while none
of them actually reaches the goal" (*RR*, p. 129).

Barth's position is similar to Brunner's, but he carries it out on
a grander scale. He believes that Luther and Calvin saw the
unity of Scripture and theology in Jesus Christ but failed to
carry this ideal out programmatically. And he claims that
Schleiermacher showed how all of theology could be harmonized
under one dominant principle. Barth takes Calvin and Luther's
Christocentrism, and Schleiermacher's systematic methodology
and attempts to write a theology harmonized around a Christology. Every doctrine — creation, providence, theodicy, anthropology — is Christologically treated. But Barth does not want
to admit to any kind of Hegelian systematizing, so he says that
it is not a doctrine about Jesus Christ that is the center of
theology, but the living Lord Jesus Christ Himself.

UNIVERSALISM

Universalism is the doctrine which teaches that all men are
God's children and that He will not rest until He has saved them
all. Cauthen notes that liberalism gave up the distinction of
saved and lost, and under the doctrine of the brotherhood of
man considered all men children of God (*IARL*). All men
are immortal and continue in the next life the spiritual development begun in this life.

Brunner surveys this doctrine briefly, noting that the first
universalist was Origen (*D*, I, 352ff.). Schleiermacher, the
founder of religious liberalism, was in principle a universalist.
According to Brunner we cannot preach universalism. We can
only preach the decision of faith in Jesus Christ. Nor can we
speculate about those who have not heard. We cannot accept
the doctrine of double predestination nor can we accept the doctrine of universalism. Our sole responsibility is to confront men
with the gospel and not attempt to think through to a logically
satisfying theory of the fate of those who do not believe.

Nels Ferré has argued for a universalism on the grounds that
God is pure, holy Love, and He would be disappointed if any
child of His were not redeemed. He reacts quite strongly to a
doctrine of hell which to him is a denial of the love of God (*SU*,
p. 34). Again, "No, the sovereign Lord is saving Love, and

134

shall win His full victory within His own eternal time" (*ibid.*).

Barth has been accused of universalism on the basis of his doctrines of election and justification. According to Barth Jesus
Christ bore the rejection of all men and therefore in principle
no man will face a rejection at a last judgment. Furthermore
when God elected Christ as The Man of election he elected the
entire race; and when God justified Christ in the resurrection he
justified all men. The logical inference seems to be that all men
are elect, justified, and therefore saved. But Barth does not draw
this conclusion. He seems to say that it would infringe the
freedom of God to claim that at this present time all men are
saved, or any other such statement. Only God knows the decision
and he knows it in his freedom; therefore, it is outside our speculation. Others interpret Barth as saying that all men are saved,
but a man may cancel his salvation. Thus evangelism is inform-
ing people that they are saved, imploring them to live as Christians, and beseeching them not to renounce their salvation in
Christ.

UNPROVABILITY

Bultmann believes that the area of that which is provable is
the territory of some positive science. Therefore theological
assertions cannot be provable, for then they would be competing
with some specific science. Hence theological statements are
unverifiable (*E*, pp. 18f.).

VENTURE

Brunner has stressed faith as venture. Faith is not prompted
by evidences nor logical consistency. There is no earthly security
for the free address of God to man in Jesus Christ, and man
must respond with the venture of faith. Brunner says that faith
always appears to unbelief as venture (*RR*, p. 187). To the
Christian it does not appear as a bold leap against the evidences,
but as a gift. The believer therefore says, "I can do no other."

VIRGIN BIRTH

Brunner makes a distinction between the fact of the incarnation, which he accepts, and the explanation of the incarnation,
namely, the virgin birth, which he does not accept (*TM*, pp.

322-327). Furthermore, the true humanity of Christ demands a human father. The virgin birth is the church's biological speculation about the mechanics of the incarnation. According to Brunner, it is improper and to be rejected. The virgin birth does not protect the incarnation for a heretic such as Paul of Samosata believed it. In his *Dogmatics* (II, 352ff.) he again attacks the virgin birth, suggesting that John's Gospel corrects Matthew and Luke.

Barth has replied with a vigorous defense of the virgin birth against Brunner's attack (*CD*, I/2, 172-202). Barth does not believe that Christ's virgin birth was a protection from sin, but that it was the sign of the incarnation. In essence, Barth's position is that if Jesus would have had a human father the incarnation would always be suspect. By being born of a virgin he has a humanity which was not produced as humanity is reproduced in the on-going of the generations, but has a humanity directly from God. Thus the virgin birth is vital to the doctrine of the incarnation. H. E. W. Turner sides with Barth against Brunner ("The Virgin Birth," *XT*, 28:2-17, Oct. 1960).

WITNESS OF THE SPIRIT, *see* Spirit, Witness of

WHOLLY OTHER, *see* Other, Wholly; *Deus Absconditus*

WORD OF GOD

The old post-Reformation orthodox theologians used the expression "the word of God" for all the revelations of God. They affirmed that the Scriptures were one form of the word of God. But in the passage of time the term narrowed down so that it was used exclusively of the Scriptures. Thus, among contemporary fundamentalists, evangelicals, and orthodox, the expression "word of God" stands for Sacred Scripture.

In neo-orthodoxy the expression has suffered from inflation. However, both Barth and Brunner agree that in the most original sense the expression "the Word of God" stands for God Himself in his self-revelation, and that Jesus Christ is peculiarly the Word of God in that He is the Son of God manifest in the flesh. Barth writes "God's Word is God Himself in His revelation" (*CD*, I/1, 339). Concerning Christ he writes: "Jesus Christ is therefore the real and active Revealer of God and Reconciler with God, because in Him, His Son or Word, God sets and gives to be known. . . . He is the Son or the Word of God for us, because He was so previously in Himself" (*ibid.*, p. 476).

Brunner writes: "This certainty that the Bible is the Word of God is, however, only possible so long as we understand by the Word of God nothing other than Christ Himself the [King and Lord of Scripture], and the Scripture as the 'crib wherein Christ lieth'" (*RR*, p. 169n).

Both Barth and Brunner allow the Bible to be called the Word of God in an indirect sense, *i.e.*, not as the revelation itself but as the witness or pointer to revelation. Thus Brunner writes: "The Scriptures are the Word of God, because and in so far as, they give us Christ . . . For the object of faith is nothing other than God Himself, in His revealing and redeeming action" (*ibid.*, p. 280). Barth entitles an entire section of his discussion "The Written Word of God" (*CD*, I/1, 111ff.).

Tillich finds six different meanings to the expression "word of God" (*ST*, I, 157ff.). (1) The word of God means that God as the ground of being is the source of the word about himself. (2) The word of God is the creative word, the medium of creation. (3) The word of God is the revelatory acts of God in the history of revelation. (4) The word of God is the manifestation in the life of Jesus Christ who is Jesus as the Christ. (5) The Scriptures as the final document of revelation are the word of God. (6) The preaching and teaching of the church can be called the word of God.

Tillich concludes: "The many different meanings of the term 'Word' are all united in one meaning, namely, 'God manifest' — manifest in himself, in creation, in the history of revelation, in the final revelation, in the Bible, in the word of the Church and her members. 'God manifest' — the mystery of the divine abyss expresses itself through the divine Logos — this is the meaning of the symbol, the 'Word of God'" (*ibid.*, p. 159).

Bultmann seems to invest the word of God and preaching with a kind of existential power. In fact he has a real philosophy and theology of the word of God. It is God's address to us of his love and forgiveness in Christ which when believed by us becomes an event (cf. *JW*, pp. 216ff.).

Contemporary evangelical theology is insistent upon calling the Scriptures the Word of God in the primary sense in that they are the inspired document of special revelation. Because they are the inspired document of revelation they participate in the structure or constellation of revelation and rightly deserve the title, "The Word of God" (cf. Ramm, *RWG*, chap. 8; Henry [ed.], *RB*).

WORLD PICTURE, WORLD VIEW

A world picture is the model we use in putting together our experiences of space, time, events, and matter. Thus Newton's and Einstein's cosmology are world pictures.

A world view is a definite theory of the metaphysical character of the universe. Pantheism, materialism, and idealism are world views.

Bultmann does not believe that Christianity gives us a world view (*E*, pp. 6-9; *JCM*, p. 83). World views are always externalizations and objectifications. Thus they in principle compete with world pictures. But Christianity as kerygma resolves the problem of a new understanding and is not an externalized nor objectified world view.

Furthermore, Bultmann takes the world picture of the New Testament to be the world view of the New Testament. It is therefore in stark contradiction to the world picture of Einstein under which modern man lives. It is mythological, and it must be demythologized in order that Christianity be understood as the achievement of a new self-understanding and not the achievement of a world view.

LIST OF ABBREVIATIONS

AC	S. Kierkegaard, *Attack Upon "Christendom"*
AP	C. H. Dodd, *The Apostolic Preaching*
APC	Leon Morris, *The Apostolic Preaching of the Cross*
APT	Aubrey Johnson, *Authority in Protestant Theology*
BCR	Paul K. Jewett, *Emil Brunner's Concept of Revelation*
BDT	Everett Harrison (ed.), *Baker's Dictionary of Theology*
BFCF	Edwin Lewis, *The Biblical Faith and Christian Freedom*
BG	C. H. Dodd, *The Bible and the Greeks*
BWT	James Baar, *Biblical Words for Time*
CA	Alan Richardson, *Christian Apologetics*
CD	Karl Barth, *Church Dogmatics*
COD	S. Kierkegaard, *The Concept of Dread*
COT	Edward J. Carnell, *The Case for Orthodox Theology*
CQ	George Ladd, *Crucial Questions About the Kingdom of God*
CR	Reinhold Niebuhr, *Christian Realism*
CT	Oscar Cullmann, *Christ and Time*
CTLP	L. Harold DeWolf, *The Case for Theology in a Liberal Perspective*
CUP	S. Kierkegaard, *Concluding Unscientific Postscript*
D	Emil Brunner, *Dogmatics*
E	Rudolf Bultmann, *Essays*
EF	Rudolf Bultmann, *Existence and Faith*
ENNTP	Robert Mounce, *The Essential Nature of New Testament Preaching*
EOR	Vergilius Ferm, *An Encyclopedia of Religion*
ER	Carl F. H. Henry, *Evangelical Responsibility in Contemporary Theology*
ET	John Macquarrie, *An Existentialist Theology*
FCC	Gustave Aulén, *The Faith of the Christian Church*

List of Abbreviations

FT	S. Kierkegaard, *Fear and Trembling*
GV	Austin Farrer, *The Glass of Vision*
HCT	Marvin Halverson and Arthur Cohen (eds.), *A Handbook of Christian Theology*
HE	Rudolf Bultmann, *History and Eschatology*
HT	Jerald Brauer, *A Handbook of Theology*
IAB	Benjamin Warfield, *The Inspiration and Authority of the Bible*
IARL	Kenneth Cauthen, *The Impact of American Religious Liberalism*
IAT	Martin Buber, *I and Thou*
IB	J. C. K. von Hofmann, *Interpreting the Bible*
IDB	*The Interpreter's Dictionary of the Bible*
IGM	David Cairns, *The Image of God in Man*
IR	John Baillie, *The Idea of Revelation*
IRD	A. Lecerf, *Introduction to Reformed Dogmatics*
ISRD	Oscar Cullmann, *Immortality of the Soul or Resurrection of the Dead?*
JBL	*Journal of Biblical Literature*
JCM	Rudolf Bultmann, *Jesus Christ and Mythology*
JW	Rudolf Bultmann, *Jesus and the Word*
KA	R. Bretall, *A Kierkegaard Anthology*
KB	Bouillard, *Karl Barth*
KH	Ellwein, *Kerygma and History*
KM	H. Bartsch and R. Fuller (eds.), *Kerygma and Myth*
KPR	Reidar Thomte, *Kierkegaard's Philosophy of Religion*
LOCT	John Cobb, *Living Options in Contemporary Theology*
MHE	L. Gilkey, *Maker of Heaven and Earth*
MIR	Emil Brunner, *Man in Revolt*
MW	Emil Brunner, *The Mystic and the Word*
NDM	Reinhold Niebuhr, *The Nature and Destiny of Man*
NE	R. Lightner, *Neo-Evangelicalism*
NM	C. VanTil, *The New Modernism*

List of Abbreviations

ODCC	*The Oxford Dictionary of the Christian Church*
PBI	Bernard Ramm, *Protestant Biblical Interpretation*
PC	G. C. Berkouwer, *The Person of Christ*
PCR	Edward J. Carnell, *A Philosophy of the Christian Religion*
PF	S. Kierkegaard, *Philosophical Fragments*
PHOT	Hans Meyerhoff, *Philisophy of History in Our Time*
PST	Abraham Kuyper, *Principles of Sacred Theology*
PR	Emil Brunner, *The Philosophy of Religion*
R	Baillie and Martin (eds.), *Revelation*
RB	Carl F. H. Henry (ed.), *Revelation and the Bible*
RHR	Richard R. Niebuhr, *Resurrection and Historical Reason*
RLR	H. Wieman, *et. al.*, *Religious Liberals Reply*
RR	Emil Brunner, *Revelation and Reason*
RRR	L. Harold DeWolf, *The Religious Revolt Against Reason*
RT	Horton, *Realistic Theology*
RWG	Bernard Ramm, *Special Revelation and the Word of God*
SC	Nels Ferré, *Swedish Contributions to Modern Theology*
ST	Paul Tillich, *Systematic Theology*
SU	Nels Ferré, *The Sun and the Umbrella*
SUD	S. Kierkegaard, *The Sickness unto Death*
TCERK	*Twentieth-Century Encyclopedia of Religious Knowledge*
TM	Emil Brunner, *The Mediator*
TMT	D. Macintosch, *Types of Modern Theology*
TNT	Rudolf Bultmann, *The Theology of the New Testament*
TPT	Kegley and Bretall, *The Theology of Paul Tillich*
TT	*Theology Today*
TWB	Alan Richardson *A Theological Word Book of the Bible*
TWNT	G. Kittel and G. Friedrich, *Theologisches Wörterbuch zum Neuen Testament*
WI	L. Mascall, *Words and Images*
WS	Bernard Ramm, *The Witness of the Spirit*
XT	*Expository Times*

141